Social Work
RECLAIMED

of related interest

Good Practice in Safeguarding Children
Working Effectively in Child Protection
Edited by Liz Hughes and Hilary Owen
ISBN 978 1 84310 945 7
Good Practice in Health, Social Care and Criminal Justice series

Safeguarding Children Across Services
Messages from Research
Carolyn Davies and Harriet Ward
ISBN 978 1 84905 124 8
Safeguarding Children Across Services series

Caring for Abused and Neglected Children
Making the Right Decisions for Reunification or Long-Term Care
Jim Wade, Nina Biehal, Nicola Farrelly and Ian Sinclair
ISBN 978 1 84905 207 8
Safeguarding Children Across Services series

Recognizing and Helping the Neglected Child
Evidence-Based Practice for Assessment and Intervention
Brigid Daniel, Julie Taylor and Jane Scott
Foreword by Enid Hendry
ISBN 978 1 84905 093 7
Safeguarding Children Across Services series

Relationship-Based Social Work
Getting to the Heart of Practice
Edited by Gillian Ruch, Danielle Turney and Adrian Ward
ISBN 978 1 84905 003 6

The Child's World
The Comprehensive Guide to Assessing Children in Need
2nd edition
Edited by Jan Horwath
ISBN 978 1 84310 568 8

Social Work with Children and Families
Getting into Practice
3rd edition
Ian Butler and Caroline Hickman
ISBN 978 1 84310 598 5

Good Practice in Assessing Risk
Current Knowledge, Issues and Approaches
Edited by Hazel Kemshall and Bernadette Wilkinson
ISBN 978 1 84905 059 3
Good Practice in Health, Social Care and Criminal Justice series

Edited by
Steve Goodman
and **Isabelle Trowler**

Social Work
RECLAIMED

Innovative Frameworks for Child
and Family Social Work Practice

Foreword by Eileen Munro

Jessica Kingsley *Publishers*
London and Philadelphia

First published in 2012
by Jessica Kingsley Publishers
116 Pentonville Road
London N1 9JB, UK
and
400 Market Street, Suite 400
Philadelphia, PA 19106, USA

www.jkp.com

Library of Congress Cataloging in Publication Data
A CIP catalog record for this book is available from the Library of Congress

British Library Cataloguing in Publication Data
A CIP catalogue record for this book is available from the British Library

ISBN 978 1 84905 202 3
eISBN 978 0 85700 461 1

Printed and bound in Great Britain

In memory of Debra Philip – forever present
October 11th 1953 to September 9th 2010

Contents

Foreword

This book offers an exciting and persuasive account of how children and their families can receive better help from social workers. It relates how two social workers became so shocked by the poor quality of the social work they saw that they became determined to work out how to run a service that could offer effective help to children, young people and their families.

As I analysed in my review of child protection for the Coalition Government (Munro 2011), previous efforts to reform social work with children and families, though individually intelligent, had combined to create an unbalanced system where compliance with performance indicators and procedures had slowly eroded the space for professional, creative work. Bureaucratic demands and rigid timescales were hindering social workers from engaging constructively and flexibly with families. Persistent media criticism had demoralised many and encouraged defensive practice.

In the comedy *Yes Minister*, the senior civil servant tells the Minister he is being 'courageous' when he means he is being reckless and doomed to failure. Steve Goodman and Isabelle Trowler looked 'courageous' to many when they decided to challenge the trend and reclaim social work as a skilled helping profession. The chapters in this book illustrate how well they have succeeded.

Written by those working in different parts of the service, they provide fascinating accounts of working with families. In each, there is a vivid tale about practice, showing the emotional impact of the work and the depth of thinking needed to help families shift their patterns of behaviour. Media coverage of social work is almost exclusively critical. The public have only heard stories where social workers are deemed to have got it wrong, often because they are, allegedly, stupid, lazy or callous. These chapters offer a wonderful contrast, depicting the motivation and enthusiasm of the workers and the challenging nature of the work, demanding high levels of intellectual and emotional intelligence.

I joined the social work profession in the 1970s when it seemed a profession with an exciting future. It has been sad to see over the decades how its reputation has faltered and its workforce has lost morale. Now, the tide is turning. The Reclaiming Social Work model was successful in the old system but, it is hoped, it will be easier for others to follow suit now that radical reforms are being implemented in England. The Social Work Taskforce (2009) report and my review of child protection (Munro 2011) have helped to refocus attention on developing professional expertise to help families. Revisions to social work training, reductions in the degree of centralised prescription, and changes to the criteria and methods of inspection should help social work agencies to make the journey from a compliant to a learning organisation where the experiences and outcomes of children are the key feedback data that shape the work. This book shows one successful way of reforming social work to produce not just a happier workforce but, more importantly, happier children, young people and families.

Eileen Munro
Professor of Social Policy
London School of Economics and Political Science

References

Munro E. (2011) *The Munro Review of Child Protection: Final Report. A Child-centred System*. London: Department for Education. Available at www.education.gov.uk/publications/eOrderingDownload/Munro-Review.pdf, accessed on 20 September 2011.

Social Work Taskforce (2009) *Building a Safe, Confident Future: The Final Report of the Social Work Task Force*. London: DCSF.

CHAPTER 1

Introduction

Isabelle Trowler and Steve Goodman

From design to delivery, the last six years has seen the development of a completely different operational system for child and family statutory social work on the front line. 'Reclaiming Social Work' is a well-known model across the UK and has also earned an international reputation. In 2010 the Human Reliability Associates and London School of Economics and Political Science (LSE) evaluation (Cross, Hubbard and Munro 2010) found that the model had produced an organisational culture of reflective learning and skill development, openness and support and most importantly, the re-establishment of a family focus within statutory social work. It also found significant evidence of better decision-making, improved interaction with families and professionals, better consistency and continuity of care, a reduction of constraints on practice and a significant reduction in the burden of administration on practice. Definitive positive outcomes included a reduction in overall costs, a significant reduction in the number of children coming into public care (40 per cent), a 50 per cent reduction in staff sickness levels and a reduction in the use of agency staff, from 50 to 7 per cent.

In the Coalition Government's *Munro Review of Child Protection: Final Report. A Child-centred System*, published in 2011 (Munro 2011), the Reclaiming Social Work model was heralded as a best practice design.

This book sets out the story of Reclaiming Social Work, and describes the detail of the operational system. Chapter 2 offers a detailed look at how systems theory has been applied to the design, implementation and review of the model. Chapters 3 and 4 discuss, respectively, the application of systemic family therapy and social learning theory (SLT) to child and family social work. Chapters 5 through to 10 offer a series of personal accounts of working as consultant social workers with case responsibility for families, with case examples of the model in practice.

Chapter 11 offers the perspective of a children's practitioner who arrived in Hackney when the model was just starting to be implemented and who still practises there today. Finally, Chapter 12 offers the personal perspective of the co-creators of the model, and describes the moment of conception of the model and through the change journey.

Traditional child and family social work operational systems are usually made up of teams of social workers, typically supervised by a team manager. Often a team manager supervises seven or eight workers, each of whom carries a caseload of children and families. Caseload numbers vary considerably depending on the type of work being undertaken, and the complexity of individual casework. It is not uncommon, however, for a team manager to have responsibility for over 100 children. The social worker is allocated the case and is provided with case direction by the team manager. The social worker visits the family and implements the agreed plan. The social worker reports back to the team manager, usually on an ad hoc day-to-day basis, and more formally through supervision typically held every four to six weeks. Teams have a variety of management and administration arrangements in place to support them in their work. Most often a middle manager is responsible for three or four team managers, and each team has access to one or two administrators. The bulk of administration arising from casework is undertaken by the allocated social worker.

The job of social work is a challenging one, requiring a range of complex skills and a sound knowledge base from which to practise. This includes the skills and knowledge to carry out comprehensive risk assessments and the implementation of effective interventions. Social workers need to understand both the physical and emotional development of children, young people and adults, and have the ability to form positive relationships with families and other professionals.

Often, the challenge for social work is to effect positive change in children's lives within the poverty and deprivation that many families live and the discrimination that many families face on a day-to-day basis. The needs of the families are hugely diverse and responses must be tailored to individual need and family circumstances. However, there are clearly some very striking and frequently presenting features of our casework. Adult health and behaviours are central to understanding parenting capacity which is limited often, and to a greater or lesser extent, by parental mental ill health, learning difficulties, drug and alcohol misuse and domestic violence. These behaviours often lead to dysfunctional and chaotic family circumstances which result in children's needs not being met. How to identify and assess need and risk, and how to provide help within complex family contexts and limited resources, needs a very particular set of personal qualities as well as professional knowledge and skill.

Chapter 2 describes in more detail the model's operational functioning, but the book as a whole offers an insight into a system that does things differently. The need to do things differently arises from a robust critique of the traditional system.

The team manager, often responsible for scores of children in high risk, high need environments, makes decisions about statutory action and support, most often without setting eyes on the child, family or home environment. Over time the team manager becomes reliant on the social worker's perspective on what is happening within the family. The pressures within statutory teams are often immense and volume of work unpredictable, and the capacity of the team manager and social worker to sit down and engage in thoughtful, reflective dialogue is commonly significantly restricted.

One of the key reasons that capacity is so stretched is the amount of administration needing to be processed. This has been increasingly the case since a focus on performance management regimes has outweighed the value placed on direct work with families. Public accountability has been sought through an endless paper trail detailing activity and process rather than a focus on evidence-based intervention and positive outcomes for families.

Reclaiming Social Work has completely redesigned who does what within the child and family social work system. Administration is undertaken by administrators. Practitioners spend most of their time with families, and they have the authority to make decisions and spend money. The organisation trusts its practitioners to use their professional judgement and skill in managing risk and keeping children safe, and management activity is designed to support practitioners in their task of creating optimal conditions to enable good practice to flourish.

References

Cross, S., Hubbard, A. and Munro, E. (2010) *Reclaiming Social Work: London Borough of Hackney Children and Young People's Services, Parts 1 and 2.* London: Human Reliability Associates and London School of Economics and Political Science.

Munro E. (2011) *The Munro Review of Child Protection: Final Report. A Child-centred System.* London: Department for Education. Available at www.education.gov.uk/publications/ eOrderingDownload/Munro-Review.pdf, accessed on 20 September 2011.

A Systems Methodology for Child and Family Social Work

Isabelle Trowler and Steve Goodman

This chapter sets out the detail underpinning the 7S conceptual framework (see below) we used to help us understand and remain focused on the different components of the Reclaiming Social Work practice system. Attention to the whole system is necessary for effective practice, and that attention must continue in order to keep the practice system constantly in balance. Knowing that each sub-system interacts and impacts on practice in varying ways over time is critical. It requires careful observation and a leadership position (at all levels) of always *knowing* the organisation. Where part of the system begins to go out of kilter, the need to think through why and what will re-balance that system most effectively and speedily is essential.

The 7S framework

The 7S framework helps conceptualise all the different components that need attention if a whole systems change has a chance of being successful. The basic premise of the 7S framework (sometimes known as the McKinsey model) is that there are seven internal aspects of an organisation that need to be aligned if the organisation is to be successful.

These seven interdependent factors (where a change in one affects all the others) are categorised as either 'hard' or 'soft' elements. 'Hard' elements (*strategy, structure, systems*) are easier to define or identify and management can directly influence them. These are, for example, strategy statements, organisation charts and reporting lines, and formal processes, procedures and IT systems. 'Soft' elements (*shared values, skills, staff, style*), on the other hand, can be more difficult to describe, and are less tangible and more influenced by culture. These 'soft' elements are, however, as important as the 'hard' elements if the organisation is going to be successful.

The model is based on the theory that, for an organisation to perform well, the seven elements need to be aligned and mutually reinforcing, so the model can be used to help identify what needs to be realigned to improve performance or to maintain alignment (and performance) during other types of change. The seven factors are depicted as a matrix, with shared values in the centre.

All statutory child and family social work services have, at some stage, undergone change programmes to address specific practice or management deficits, with varying success – small-scale and incremental changes will always change some things. However, the tendency has been to create well-intentioned structures or tools thought to have the potential to help improve practice but which often fail because at a national and local level not enough attention is given to the impact on the whole system, and what else may need to change to create success. Attempts to enhance front-line practice skills by creating new quality assurance roles or models of intervention frequently and, despite attempts to do otherwise, ultimately lie outside the main practice system, perceived by front-line practitioners as something other, for which they have to ask permission to access. These add-on and separate practice systems become homes for expert preciousness, often draining the supply of the most skilled, experienced and confident workers away from casework priorities. Existing systems that need to change will only do so if improvement strategies are mainstreamed. Where entrenched problems within a profession have led to systems failure, nothing less than a *whole* systems change will create fundamental and sustainable progress.

The 7S framework simply shows the key interdependent elements present within organisations, providing us with a road map for change management.

Our shared values

Critical to the success of Reclaiming Social Work was establishing a shared value base from which to work. In the often stressful, high risk and highly active environment that is statutory child and family social work, it is all too easy to lose sight of our purpose and our values. This is often illustrated by a tendency to behave in punitive, risk-averse ways towards some of the most vulnerable children and families in our society. Fundamentally, Reclaiming Social Work is primarily interested in keeping children safely together with their families wherever possible, limiting the role of the state in families' lives and, when that role needs to be executed, that it is done speedily, with depth and decisiveness. Reclaiming Social Work is underpinned by a perspective on social disadvantage and discrimination and seeks to articulate the major impact this has on every aspect of life. Too often in the past it is possible to see how professional stories that have been built around families and their children have lacked substance, often a result of value-laden assessments and judgements being made.

Judgements made about families must always be made within a context of emotional intelligence and empathy. While holding the safety of the child in mind, we must work in partnership with parents, an often forgotten concept embedded by the Children Act 1989. In our work with families we need to stop, listen and think about what has been said and the meaning this has for the child's welfare. Reclaiming Social Work seeks to create and support a practice system in which practitioners are proud of the work they do and willing to take responsibility and own the impact they have on families' futures. Social workers are very powerful professionals, and threatening to families by their very presence. The practice system should enable practitioners to be confident in the positions they take, and for them to have the courage and integrity to admit that sometimes they are wrong. This can be done best by an organisational culture that accepts that mistakes will be made, and when this happens, not focus on blame towards the individual but on enhancing the operating systems so that the risk of repeat error is reduced.

Reclaiming Social Work is a method of practice that is fundamentally connected with collaborative and respectful working, inviting the family and all the members of the system (including the professionals and others in the child's wider system, from family, to school and other services) to join in finding a solution to the presenting difficulty. In this way professionals are not seen to have all the answers, but instead look to the family's own understanding and particular knowledge of what is not working, and help them to identify and build on their own skills to create a way to move forward. By privileging the voices of parents/carers and children and those involved in their lives, Reclaiming Social Work provides a context in which families gain enough confidence to rely on their own strengths and resiliencies to play a greater role in finding a solution. In general family systems are self-regulating and can manage most difficulties on their own, or with minimal support. This is the everyday resilience by which most families survive the challenges they encounter over time. Where intervention is required, however brief, social workers must question some of the problem-saturated descriptions that tend to accompany referrals as a way of liberating professional energy and attention towards solution and sustained change.

The practice value system described here must be supported through organisational behaviours. The driver for decisions on who does what within the organisation should be the interests of children and families, and not dictated by procedural and/or service specifications. The latter are there to guide, not to bind us. Senior leadership behaviours within local authorities must be directed towards practice concerns, with a visible and active interest in casework progression and effectiveness. Time used up in unnecessary bureaucracy is time taken away from managing front-line operations and the risks that exist for children within it.

Partnership, too, with other professionals, is critical. It is hard enough for families to have a number of different people with different professional perspectives impacting on their family life without the relationships between those professionals being fractious, competitive and mutually dismissive. Unfortunately in the past this kind of interaction would not be unusual. Reclaiming Social Work promotes the utmost respect for the other professionals we work with, and encourages the resolution of differences and tensions far away from our interactions with families.

Our strategy

Reclaiming has always been described as a change agenda of three to five years. There are no quick fixes, but the strategy in one sense is simple — we need the right people in the organisation who have a high level of skill and who are interested and able to identify and manage risk and design and deliver family interventions that work. Strategic management of the development of the staff group by building a sufficiently effective skills base requires a prescriptive approach to intervention methodology. This enables a dedicated focus on a chosen skill set and a select menu of interventions that will then be delivered to a high standard, rather than the historical scattergun approach to practice traditionally seen in statutory child and family social work services. With an evidence-based range of interventions and a staff group who are equipped to build positive relationships with children and families, and provided with frequent and systematic opportunities to be reflective and thoughtful about the intention and impact of direct work, more families are more likely to be able to successfully change their behaviours sufficiently to keep their children safely at home.

Numbers of children in public care will steadily reduce. This will release significant resources from commissioning budgets that can, in part, be identified for efficiency savings for the authority as well as providing an opportunity to invest money into early intervention services, helping families earlier.

A practice system which is effective in its work to safeguard children and support families will be a system in which practitioners will want to work, and stay. This will generate day-to-day satisfaction and continuity of casework, a culture of support and learning, and therefore less turnover, less drift and less firefighting. It will create opportunity and expectation to engage constantly in thoughtful and effective social work.

Our structure: the social work unit

Consultant
social
worker

Social
worker

Family
therapist/
clinical
practitioner

Children's
practitioner

Unit
coordinator

Figure 2.2 The social work unit

Hackney was the first statutory child and family social work department in England to introduce small multi-disciplinary social work units as a way of supporting families towards change using prescriptive methodologies for interventions. While many authorities have boutique-type projects doing similar work and with a similar skills set, all casework in Hackney is managed through this arrangement. The evidence-based skills set and multi-disciplinary approach has been mainstreamed. Having a range of professionals available in the units means practitioners are able to provide a service for children and their families using the expertise of different disciplines and perspectives, with direct lines of communication to more specialist services if such a need is identified.

Each of the units is led by a consultant social worker, who has, working alongside them, another social worker, a children's practitioner, a unit coordinator and a clinician (a systemic family therapist or a clinical practitioner in training to be so). In general, the units discuss all the children allocated to the unit on a weekly basis, agreeing tasks with the consultant social worker who has overall case responsibility. The model encourages greater continuity of care for families, with no child reliant on one member of staff for their support. In the absence of one worker there is always another who will know what is happening for the family. Holiday, sickness, staff vacancy or court proceedings are managed without casework stopping in the absence of the allocated worker.

The unit meeting is also the main mechanism for case supervision, that is, discussion, debate, reflection and decision-making. Group managers, who line manage the consultants, regularly attend unit meetings so they can hear and judge the quality of professional discussion and decision-making. Group managers do meet with consultants but this tends to be more focused on the pastoral and professional development of the consultant rather than casework supervision, although of course those conversations can and do take place. Consultants also have opportunities for case consultation outside of the unit expertise and that provided by the group manager through the head of psychology, the head of systemic practice, the head of safeguarding, and weekly sessions provided by an adult psychiatrist. The culture of the organisation is one where the consultant is proactive in seeking the advice and support they need. The onus is on the practitioner to identify what they don't know and to seek additional expertise and case consultation. The practice system is designed so that those opportunities are available and easily accessible.

The group manager's key task is to provide optimal conditions for enabling social work units to flourish. Of course group managers will be available to discuss complex cases but they are also charged with helping to create an infrastructure and an associated culture that supports and develops the units.

Unit coordinators also have a critical role in making life as easy as possible for practitioners. They need to be very proactive, thinking ahead of the game and finding solutions before the others in the unit even know there is a problem. They lead on diary management and do all data entry; they organise meetings (venues, invites, etc.); set up children's medicals, dental appointments and holiday activities; make sure the right papers are available in the right format at the right time; record case discussion and decisions taken in the unit meetings directly onto children's files; sort out basic things for children, young people and families; and devise and support systems which enable the unit to track timescales for statutory visits, reviews, court directions, etc.

Structure is important and it does make a difference. However, the roles within that structure are fluid and tasks are allocated to individuals on the basis of what needs to get done for families and when, experience, skills set and practice interest. There is no room in this structure for anyone to say 'that's not my job'. Practitioners and managers work together to do what needs to be done.

Our systems

This refers to the procedures, processes and routines that characterise how the work should be done: childcare decision-making; financial systems; recruitment and performance appraisal systems; and information systems. In essence systems should be simple so that they are relevant, intelligent, flexible and useful to practitioners. Anything that an organisation creates should only exist to facilitate effective working with families. Anything that exists which hampers effective practice should be quickly changed or stopped altogether.

Procedures should be limited with practitioners encouraged to think through what they want to do and why, and then do it, rather than do it because they are told to. Too many rules lead to a mechanistic, managerial-led response to professional social work practice. Some rules are essential, of course, particularly in the context of working across agencies so that expectations are clear, but any procedure should be brief, instructive and to the point.

A heavy focus on information technology as a tool for practice has, to date, encouraged fragmented thinking with reduced capacity to tell the story of the child and the family. In a different context these tools may have had more potential, but without a sophisticated and intellectually robust profession to receive and use them, their implementation has been to the detriment of practice.

Key to the success of Reclaiming Social Work has been to think through all key decisions and to bring the authority for decision-making as close to the family as possible. Nearly all decisions are held at consultant level, although financial decisions are taken closer to families, and the most junior members of units have authority to spend money. For years families and young people have told us how frustrating it is to hear their social worker say they have to go and ask their manager for something as simple as spending £20. Reclaiming Social Work promotes the need to trust staff. Since devolvement of spending decisions in Hackney, the Section 17 spend[1] has actually reduced, not increased. Where dubious spending decisions have been made, and these are very rare, that is managed by exception, rather than operating a system that assumes poor and reckless decision-making as standard. This more traditional deficit approach to practice is counter-productive.

Separating children from their families either through voluntary agreement with parents or through care proceedings is such a monumental decision in a child's life that Reclaiming Social Work believes this is one decision which should be made using the collective wisdom of a range of people and ultimately taken by senior leaders. A weekly resource panel, usually chaired by the assistant director and attended by consultants, heads of service and the principal lawyer, can also help to ensure that where there is a significant chance that, with a coordinated care plan, children can safely remain with their parents or extended networks, the resources required to do this are properly mobilised. In essence the panel shares an informed responsibility for separating families and shares the risk when decisions are made to keep children with families or extended family.

Undoing years of red tape is a time-consuming and laborious and often fractious task. Local authorities must have transparent systems for

---

1   Section 17 of the Children Act 1989 places a duty on local authorities to provide services for children in need, their families and others.

public accountability and senior leaders have to identify ways of reducing bureaucracy that don't undermine this essential requirement. For progress to be made, senior officers need to be determined to get it right for front-line services and for families.

Our style

Reclaiming Social Work set out to do things differently, focusing on behaviours and in particular leadership behaviours at all levels of the organisation.

With regards to senior leadership, while leadership in general can be fluid and at its optimum open and diffused throughout the hierarchy, top-down leadership is sometimes very important to demonstrate. At times of organisational crisis, where an unforeseen event causes significant anxiety, for example a child death that receives a high level of media attention or when change creates tension and concern, then calm and soothing leadership from the top is essential. In the same way that social workers cannot be scared of the power vested in them in relation to families, leaders cannot ignore the power vested in senior leadership roles. That power should be utilised and visibly expressed across the system in order to effect positive systems change. Leaders need to focus on the organisational context rather than detailed operations but have and use the ability to dive in deep into the detail when needed. A strong social work senior leader will have staff from all levels of the organisation coming to talk to them and seeking their advice about casework, careers and self. This accessibility will happen because staff believe their senior leaders know them and know the organisation.

Whatever the role held, there are certain beliefs intrinsic to Reclaiming Social Work which influence and direct behaviour and generate an overall style:

- Whatever your role and wherever you are, the way you behave and the words you say or don't say send a message to those around you; that consciousness of your own power and influence is critical if it is to be used constructively and in its entirety.

- Being proactive, energised, interested and focused on change gives families the best chance of staying together and keeping children safe.

- We are all on a journey together as an organisation, and individually, and each trajectory has no final state or final position to which we must aspire; we keep on moving forwards with momentum and changing ourselves and the system we operate in for the benefit of the families we work with.

- Consistency is not the Holy Grail; there is always a myriad of different ways of thinking and doing which will result in the same desired outcome to safeguard children.

- Taking professional responsibility verbally and in writing is a key part of our approach: to own our views and actions and decisions and never to be afraid to change one's mind demonstrating that we got it wrong. Doing things differently from the mainstream is not in and of itself problematic; being thoughtful, respectful and intellectually sound in decision-making is most important and should be held in the highest regard. There is no one truth.

Our staff

Our staff are without doubt our most valuable resource and getting the right people in permanent employment in child and family statutory social work is the greatest challenge. Participating in staff selection should be given high priority by senior leaders; taking responsibility for what happens to children through social work intervention can be demonstrated by this participation.

At the time of writing there still remains huge concern about the calibre of social work students coming on to qualifying programmes, and also the variable quality and content of the teaching on university courses. While this remains the case, selection of staff becomes even more critical. All staff working within the Reclaiming Social Work model have been rigorously tested through verbal reasoning and written assessments as well as interview. These processes check for a wide range of competencies as well as attitudes, personal attributes and professional knowledge; the vast majority of applicants do not get through this process.

Statutory child and family social work is complex and demanding and to do it well, practitioners need to have a high level of skill and a strong set of personal qualities. It is absolutely critical not to compromise on competence. The impact on vulnerable families cannot be compensated for by even the most sophisticated checks and balances.

Our skills

We recognise that the job of social work is a challenging one requiring a range of complex skills and a sound knowledge base from which to practise. This includes the skills and knowledge to carry out effective assessments, to implement intervention methodologies with families which manage high risk contexts, to understand both the physical and emotional development of children and young people, the ability to make positive relationships with families and other professionals, strong report writing skills and other good communication skills. Practitioners also need to be confident, articulate and professional, and to have stamina and determination; in short, to provide an effective social work service is a difficult job. We have set high expectations of ourselves to support good social work practice and also expect staff to perform at a consistently high standard.

Reclaiming Social Work has had to develop a programme for staff which compensates for the gaps in the curriculum in social work qualification training and supports staff more generally to think and behave differently in their professional worlds as well as develop an advanced skills set for evidence-based interventions with families. We have developed strong partnerships with a number of academics and have commissioned extensive additional skills training in our preferred methodologies. This is a huge investment but we already have evidence that this expansive approach to staff development is motivating and intellectually stimulating for a group of highly intelligent and committed practitioners who want to get it right for the families with whom they work.

Conclusion

This chapter has given an overview of the conceptual framework we have used to design and support the Reclaiming Social Work practice system and some of the detail that underpins that. It seems impossible to write down everything we now know about this system, but it is hoped that this gives some insight into its intention. The realities of working within this system will be many and varied, and the chapters ahead will guide the reader to a fuller understanding. However, to know the system can only come from working within it. It is our hope that more authorities will adopt the model. For us, Reclaiming Social Work holds the future for an effective and highly regarded profession.

CHAPTER 3

Systemic Practice in a Risk Management Context

Nick Pendry

Introduction

The influence of systemic or relational thinking in the national children's statutory social care context has been increasingly evident since the publication of the *Framework for the Assessment of Children in Need and Their Families* (DoH 2000) introduced a relational frame to child protection assessments. The emphasis in this statutory guidance was on the practitioner's need to explore in the course of such assessments the interrelated domains of the child's developmental needs, parenting capacity and family and environmental factors. Think Family approaches promoted by successive governments to delivering services actively encouraged local authorities to ensure that support provided by children's, adult and family services was joined up and took account of how individual problems affect the whole family. It is within this context that Reclaiming Social Work has developed and flourished, an approach that integrates systemic practice into each area of service delivery within children's social care.

Children's social care context

The remarkable shift in emphasis in children's social care represented by Reclaiming Social Work can be fully appreciated when held against what might be viewed as the traditional understanding of child protection social work that appears to have maintained a dominant influence in practice. In this frame it would seem that child abuse is conceptualised as being based on a single causative factor. This understanding, apparently fuelled by a series of high-profile inquiries into child deaths and child sexual abuse in the 1970s and 1980s (Horwath 2001), would seem to hold the individual abuser, often the parent, as solely responsible for any harm suffered by the child. The causative factor appears somehow to reside within the parent, in the form of a mental illness, perhaps, or a problem with drug misuse, to the exclusion of any influences exerted by family and community relationships, and external stressors such as poverty or racism (Jack 1997; Stevenson 1998).

If the harm suffered by children is best understood as a result of individual pathology, it follows that attending to this parental deficit will ensure that child protection concerns are addressed. Social work intervention is targeted at the parent or carer with an emphasis on how they must change by, for instance, complying with adult mental health services, or engaging in treatment for their problematic drug misuse. These actions may initially well serve to reduce the risk of harm to the children of these parents, but the relational and contextual influences that served to result in such behaviours will remain unaddressed. Take, for example, a family in which the parental couple constantly argue, the family live in overcrowded accommodation and the parents struggle on a daily basis to clothe and feed their four children. The mother uses illegal drugs to cope with the tension and struggle of her daily life, and this leaves her often incapable of attending to her children's basic care needs. An intervention focused on this mother's drug misuse, but which fails to address her relationship with her partner, her housing and her financial situation, will leave her vulnerable to using other means to cope with her situation, and in the longer term likely to continue to neglect the needs of her children. In contrast, a systemic approach, which emphasises context and the inter-connectedness of relationships, and focuses interventions in these areas, is much more likely to achieve lasting change. This systemic understanding lies at the heart of Reclaiming Social Work.

The systemic approach

The systemic approach in practice is rooted in the discipline of family and systemic psychotherapy or family therapy, and has its theoretical roots in systems theory and cybernetics (Wiener 1961). The application of these ideas to human relationships, and in particular families, laid the foundations for family therapy, with the work of Bateson (1972, 1980) being particularly influential in view of his ideas about families being seen as cybernetic systems, and his work around the patterns of communication within family relationships. A cybernetic system was seen to be self-regulating in that it maintained stability through information looping back into a system, in order for adjustments to be made and stability maintained. Family systems would naturally strive to maintain a similar stability, or a state of homeostasis (Jackson 1957). Communication in families would serve this pull of homeostasis, with patterns of interaction between family members often following implicit family rules, such as when an argument breaks out between father and son, the mother will intervene to mediate (Hoffman 1976). This represented a shift from the psychiatric orthodoxy of the day with a view of causation being a circular process, involving a family system striving to self-regulate, rather than a linear process focused on a particular individual (Dallos and Draper 2000).

These ideas were developed into coherent theories about the particular nature of family difficulties that might result in the development of symptoms in one family member, and clear interventions that would bring about change. These models of family therapy focused variously on family structures (Minuchin 1974) in structural family therapy, family patterns of communication (Watzlawick, Weakland and Fisch 1974) in strategic family therapy and family beliefs (Palazolli *et al.* 1980) in the Milan systemic approach. Each theory held that interventions focused on the particular areas identified would bring about the required change. The integration of ideas from social constructionist theory led to the further development of the discipline with the establishment of therapeutic models such as narrative family therapy (White and Epston 1990) gaining ascendancy, with a focus on how the re-authoring of problematic family narratives might bring about family change.

The key idea that is consistent throughout this development, and so might be seen as a defining element of family therapy and which, in turn, is integral to Reclaiming Social Work, is that problems are embedded within relationships, that is, problems are understood as being interpersonal rather than intrapsychic. The mother in the example above is viewed not as having a problem that might stem from some earlier traumatic experience, which is evidenced through her problematic drug misuse and neglect of her children; rather she is seen as being involved in a set of interpersonal processes, which result in such problematic behaviour. Her current difficulties are understood within a frame of circular causality, where her actions are a response to others' actions or responses towards her, with no apparent starting point (Watzlawick *et al.* 1974). This is not to say that her actions are as influencing of, say, her partner as her partner's actions are of her; issues of power based on gender or race need to be considered. The point is that individuals who are seen as having problems are viewed as being part of a variety of relationships which are mutually influencing (Wiener 1961), and in which the specific problem behaviours identified are embedded, rather than being a result of some individual deficit.

The fit between children's social care and the systemic approach

This shift in emphasis towards a relational frame and away from an intrapsychic one can have a liberating effect on the children, young people, parents and carers who receive a service from children's social care. A child in a foster placement, for example, who is behaving in a challenging way towards their carer, and towards their teachers at school, is freed from the stigma of being seen as the problem, as the problem is understood as being embedded within their relationships at home and at school. In a similar way the social worker is liberated from searching for a way in which to fix the problem child by perhaps focusing on some idea of a disrupted early attachment relationship, and can focus instead on working with the systems in which the child is located. The problem is shared between the members of these systems, and so each member has a role to play in resolving the problem.

The influence of systemic ideas on the national children's social care context and the promotion in turn of systemic ideas as a way of meeting the requirements of this shifting emphasis seem clear. The fit between children's social care and the systemic approach is evident. Indeed the research evidence suggests that the use of systemic ideas and practice within children's social care is most likely to achieve change in working with the range of difficulties that are commonly presented within this context, such as childhood physical abuse and neglect, conduct problems in childhood and adolescence, including oppositional behaviour, difficulties and problems with attention and overactivity (Carr 2000). Family therapy is of proven effectiveness wherever it has been properly researched, and the conditions of proven effectiveness cover a wide range of difficulties (Stratton 2005). This being the case, using the systemic approach within children's social care is a clearly indicated development.

The systemic approach within Reclaiming Social Work

This development has progressed in the London Borough of Hackney through the establishment of an initial looked-after children therapy service, to a stand-alone therapeutic intervention service using a predominantly systemic approach, to a clinical service embedded within the very structure of children's social care. This service is clear about the overarching systemic emphasis which informs the delivery of the clinical service, and in turn the social work service, to children, young people and their families and carers. A key function of the clinician within the social work unit is to ensure this emphasis is maintained, a position reinforced by the ongoing systemic training undertaken by consultant social workers and other members of the social work unit. This innovative model embeds an evidence-based systemic approach into the very fabric of social work service delivery.

The apparent vulnerability of this model might be that under the immense pressure of service demand, traditional methods of practising social work might be easily fallen back on. For instance, a social worker undertaking an initial visit with a family following a child protection referral, and meeting with a father who is evidently hostile and verbally abusive to his eight-year-old son, and then to the social worker, might understandably view this father as the problem that needs to be fixed. The systems need to be in place in order to counter this thinking, and give space to a contextual and relational understanding of this family's difficulties. A systemic clinician charged with bringing this understanding into the social work unit, the social work unit meeting as a place in which such an understanding can be thought about and discussed, and the undertaking of systemic training of the social worker completing this initial visit, are just such systems that ensure these vulnerabilities are addressed.

A case example

At this point a case example can usefully illustrate the influence of the application of a systemic approach within a children's social care context.

Dean is an 11-year-old boy of white-UK ethnicity, referred to children's social care by his school. The school were concerned about Dean's interest in firearms and violence, his violent and verbally abusive outbursts at school and his mother's apparently casual attitude towards these concerns. The school described Dean as a young person who would end up in prison. His mother was talked about as being too permissive with her son, and more interested in her current partner than her son's welfare. Dean's father was not mentioned in this referral.

The referral was discussed within a social work unit meeting. The systemically trained unit clinician and the consultant social worker, undertaking a foundation year training in systemic practice, began to generate a number of systemic hypotheses (Palazolli *et al.* 1980) about this family's presenting difficulties. For example, Dean's behaviour might be seen as a response to the lack of attention he was receiving from his mother as a result of her relationship with her new partner. In this frame the family system might be experiencing a pull towards a previous stability, where Dean and his mother managed in a relatively unproblematic way. Alternatively, Dean's behaviour might be seen as a response to a lack of contact with his birth father, with the aim of encouraging his mother to bring his father back into the family system. Once again the family system might be seen as making an attempt to return to a previous relational state. Within these hypotheses the focus is removed from any apparent ideas about Dean having some internal difficulties which are showing in his current behaviour, or about his mother being somehow to blame for Dean's behaviour by her casual and permissive attitude. The family difficulties are seen as embedded within the family relationships.

The consultant social worker and the unit clinician undertook the first visit to the family home jointly. Their initial conversations with Dean and his mother focused as much on gathering relational information, in order to test out the hypotheses generated, as it did on gaining the detail of information required to complete a core assessment. This took Dean and his mother somewhat by surprise. Dean's mother talked about how she did not feel blamed by this approach, but rather was encouraged to try out relational interventions that were suggested as a way of making change in the family. Dean and his mother were encouraged to spend individual time together each week, and to prepare together what they might do in this time. Contact between Dean and his father, which had lapsed for several months, was established again. Dean, his mother and her new partner were encouraged to spend time together at home as a family, for instance watching television together or eating a meal together. At the same time direct work was undertaken with Dean around his behaviour, and Dean's mother attended an evidence-based behavioural parenting programme. This work was challenging, and at times maintaining a systemic approach was a struggle. Dean's school wanted to exclude him. Dean's mother came several times to the point where she asked for Dean to be accommodated as she could not manage his behaviour. Over several weeks, however, Dean's behaviour began to settle down, his relationship with his mother and with her new partner greatly improved, and he enjoyed his contact with his father. The core assessment was completed and there was no identified need for Dean to remain in contact with our service.

Next steps

The systemic approach is clearly a good fit with the statutory social work context of children's social care, and is an evidence-based approach that is shown to be effective in making change with a variety of presenting difficulties typical of a children's social care service. The role of the clinician in the Reclaiming Social Work model is crucial in maintaining this systemic approach in the delivery of social work across children's social care. As this approach becomes more embedded into the essence of service delivery, the development of systemic social work as a coherent model of social work practice will be achieved. This will involve social workers at all levels of the organisation using their systemic theory and practice as an integral part of their service. The supervision that they receive will similarly reflect this systemic emphasis, moving from a case management model to a systemic social work supervision, which combines a reflective-type clinical supervision with a focus on risk assessment and management. This systemic social work will represent a true paradigm shift (Kuhn 1962) in the delivery of social work services to children and young people.

References

Bateson, G. (1972) *Steps to an Ecology of Mind: Mind and Nature.* New York: Ballantine Books.

Bateson, G. (1980) *Mind and Nature: a Necessary Unity.* London: Fontana/Collins.

Carr, A. (2000) 'Evidence-based practice in family therapy and systemic consultation I: child focused problems.' *Journal of Family Therapy 22*, 29–60.

Dallos, R. and Draper, R. (2000) *An Introduction to Family Therapy: Systemic Theory and Practice*. Buckingham: Open University Press.

DoH (Department of Health) (2000) *Framework for the Assessment of Children in Need and Their Families*. London: The Stationery Office.

Hoffman, L. (1976) 'Breaking the Homeostatic Cycle.' In P. Guerin (ed.) *Family Therapy: Theory and Practice*. New York: Gardner Press.

Horwath, J. (2001) 'Assessing the World of the Child in Need: Background and Context.' In J. Horwath (ed.) *The Child's World: Assessing Children in Need. The Reader*. London: NSPCC.

Jack, G. (1997) 'Discourses of child protection and child welfare.' *British Journal of Social Work 27*, 5, 659–678.

Jackson, D. (1957) 'The question of family homeostasis.' *Psychiatry Quarterly Supplement 31*, 79–99.

Kuhn, T.S. (1962) *The Structure of Scientific Revolutions*. Chicago, IL: University of Chicago Press.

Minuchin, S. (1974) *Families and Family Therapy*. Cambridge, MA: Harvard University Press.

Palazolli, M.S., Boscolo, L., Cecchin, G. and Prata, G. (1980) 'Hypothesizing-circularity neutrality: three guidelines for the conductor of the session.' *Family Process 19*, 1, 3–12.

Stevenson, O. (1998) *Neglected Children: Issues and Dilemmas*. Oxford: Blackwell.

Stratton, P. (2005) *Report on the Evidence Base of Systemic Family Therapy*. Warrington: The Association for Family Therapy (AFT). Available at www.aft.org.uk.

Watzlawick, P., Weakland, J.H. and Fisch, R. (1974) *Change: Principles of Problem Formation and Problem Resolution*. New York: W.W. Norton.

White, M. and Epston, D. (1990) *Narrative Means to Therapeutic Ends*. New York: W.W. Norton.

Wiener, N. (1961) *Cybernetics*. Cambridge, MA: MIT Press.

CHAPTER 4

Behavioural-based Interventions

Social Learning Theory

Stewart McCafferty

This chapter is about the experience of introducing social learning theory (SLT) as practice, within a consultation framework. As this is a chapter that is first and foremost about practice, there is no detailed explanation of SLT, although there is a brief outline of the version of SLT in use in the practice described. Similarly there is no comprehensive history of SLT, nor a full set of core references; for all these, the reader is referred elsewhere. Brief theoretical/practice points are highlighted in relation to case illustrations, some of these in the discussion of the case, and some as boxes within the text.

SLT is a broad field of theory and practice, originally developed within research faculties in academic behavioural psychology. The earliest forms of it used the practice of negative (aversive) consequences as equally useful to positive (rewarding) consequences, in order to effect change in child and adult behaviour. This is unlike practice within modern SLT, where positive reinforcement of desired behaviour is the main method of influencing behavioural development. Behaviourism in psychology pre-dates psychoanalytic thinking, and developments in each have run in parallel, although almost entirely independently of one another.

My introduction to SLT was on a postgraduate social work training course, where it was the core methods course: behavioural casework. It was taught then (1980) on the basis of an established efficacy in social work as well as psychology settings. SLT has been part of my practice for many years.

SLT (see Bandura 1977; Herbert 1978, 1987) has established itself over four decades as the most effective set of interventions with children, young people and their families, where a number of life difficulties present themselves (see Box 4.1). These include: children and adolescents' emotional and behavioural difficulties, crises of harm and injury at the hands of parents and carers, as well as various mental health difficulties, for example school phobia and other phobias. These interventions are tried and tested in settings from home treatment to hospital clinic, via school, nursery and community services. They have been validated worldwide with many diverse populations and with many different professionals involved, including social work staff.

Box 4.1: Foundations of behavioural practice with parents and children

The first published accounts of behavioural work with parents and children appeared in the 1960s, alongside the development of SLT (Bandura 1977). Herbert (1978) provides a large number of citations of behavioural interventions with parents and children, from the mid-1960s onwards. Webster-Stratton and Herbert (1994) provide most of the core references from the 1970s onwards.

At first these were clinically oriented around child mental health presentations, such as repetitive minor self-harm: scratching, hair pulling. The successful application of behavioural techniques using parents as the agents of change led to applications of SLT with a wider range of child and adolescent mental health presentations as well as (following Kempe and Helfer 1968) child abuse (initially this was child battering, physical abuse).

The 1970s saw a great flourishing of family-based applications of SLT. See also Herbert (1987) for further citations.

Consequently, it made sense that SLT should be one of the main approaches to problem resolution in the new vision of children's social care that is the Reclaiming Social Work project.

Hackney children's social care is also in a minority of services within the UK in that it incorporates a tier 2 (community-based, non-medical lead) Child and Adolescent Mental Health Service (CAMHS) within children's social care (as contrasted with a tier 3 CAMHS, which is clinic-based, within the health service and led by psychiatry). It makes even better sense that SLT is one of the two core approaches, as it is one of the most widely applicable and most effective sets of interventions in CAMHS.

First of all, it might be helpful to describe the current level of SLT knowledge and experience within the children's social care service. At present, staff are trained in small cohorts in the rudiments of SLT theory in a six-day exposure. Almost none of the staff, including clinical staff, have any prior substantial SLT training, let alone experience of practice. This is as a result of two things. First, social work programmes do not teach SLT to social work students, despite its track record as the most successful model of intervention leading to significant change. Second, the children's social care service elected to recruit mostly systemic family therapists and relatively few psychologists up until now. Depending on the emphasis of the specific programme, some clinical psychologists have a good training, and solid practice experience under supervision, in SLT.

Consequent to these factors, the level of practice skills and confidence in using SLT was very low to begin with among consultation group attendees. While we might be concerned about the need for more thoroughgoing training in SLT, either within core training programmes or post-qualifying, on the other hand what this illustrates is that SLT can start to be applied by any children's social care staff who are in a position to be commissioned to undertake SLT-based practice with clients of the service.

In Hackney children's social care, as in most other children's social work/social care services in the UK, one of the key features of the social care context is the level of complexity of cases and the level of risk (and, consequently, of risk management). For instance, *The London Domestic Violence Strategy* (Mayor of London 2005) suggests that in London one in four adult partner relationships is, has been or will be violent at some point in the life span of the relationship. In a clinical (as in tier 2 or 3 CAMHS) or social care referral group, that risk is elevated, as there is a high correlation between adult on adult violence and adult on child violence, and child behaviour problems (Hazen *et al.* 2004; Kelleher *et al.* 2008; Moore and Florsheim 2008). Similarly, there is a high correlation between adult on child violence and child disability and other child factors. I would estimate that it is safe to assume that a minimum of 50 per cent of families referred to children's social care or CAMHS have domestic violence as a component of the family environment, irrespective of the denial of this. The literature on domestic violence is voluminous and presents the arguments in more detail. The reader is encouraged to explore that literature (see Box 4.2).

Box 4.2: Domestic violence

Gelles and Cornell (1990, p.23) say: 'The more dangerous acts of violence we shall refer to as "abusive violence". These acts are defined as acts that have the high potential for injuring the person being hit.'

Mullender *et al.* (2002, p.36), citing Higgins (1994), give children voice in defining domestic violence as follows:

> When your dad hits your mum and makes her cry.

> When your dad shouts, makes everyone frightened, and hurts your mum.

The second *London Domestic Violence Strategy* (Mayor of London 2005, p.11) cites a government definition:

> Any incident of threatening behaviour, violence or abuse (psychological, physical, sexual, financial or emotional) between adults who are or have been intimate partners or family members, regardless of gender or sexuality.

It states (p.vii) that domestic violence represents 25 per cent of all reported crimes of violence in London, which is seen as a vast under-report of the actual prevalence. It notes that the Metropolitan Police attend around 300 domestic violence incidents every 24 hours (p.6) and that about 75 per cent of all child protection/safeguarding referrals involve domestic violence in the family context.

Rates of denial, often under threat or duress, are very high. Women's Aid (www.womensaid.org.uk) say that 25 per cent of women in the UK will experience domestic violence at some point in their lives. The estimate in London is that 25 per cent of relationships will be violent at some point in the life of the relationship.

Practice pointer: how to interview and assess

First of all, investigation and assessment have to be seen as interventions in the family system (see, for instance, Andersen 1996; Hyden and McCarthy 1994; Mayor of London 2005). Women who are just about to speak about the domestic violence they endure are at most risk of elevated violence or murder at that moment (see Women's Aid, above), and the case is similar for women about to leave a violent relationship. This is why it is essential that professionals understand that denial of domestic violence, even in the face of obvious evidence, is a survival strategy for the woman, albeit in the short term.

It is often the case that a serially abusing partner will also exert greater and greater domination and control, partly as a feature of who they are, partly as the increased risk of law enforcement arises. This will include interrogation of the victimised partner.

This also means that separate interviewing of the abused partner (male sometimes, mostly female) needs to be conducted such that the victimised partner can account for their whereabouts and actions without giving away the fact they have spoken to a professional.

The abused partner should not be interviewed initially in the same location as the alleged abuser, let alone in the same room. Consideration also needs to be given to public locations where others who may collude with the alleged abuser may pass information should they see the victimised partner entering or leaving a public service building. It may be necessary to make initial assessment in a plausible venue, such as a medical service or an education setting, with a valid appointment there, if these agencies agree.

The assessment of domestic violence needs to gather: onset, duration, intensity, frequency, any remissions, effect on arousal states (elevated fear and flashbacks or freezing/inactivity). The timeline of domestic violence needs to be matched with onset and recurrence of child behaviour difficulties.

Once the alleged abuser accepts that openness can lead to improved outcomes for them as well as the family, then work can start with the whole family.

In our sample of children and young people referred, 100 per cent had abuse or neglect as one of the reasons for referral where the referral was accepted as a valid children's social care case. In addition to current concerns of neglect or abuse, where children are looked after by children's social care or are supported in their long-term (adoption or kinship) placements, 100 per cent of those have also experienced abuse or neglect, and often in traumatic and traumatising ways.

Further to this, to complete this brief sketch of complexity, it is quite often the case that there is a high level of traumatisation in the adult parents/carers. This is either primary, in the sense that their own childhood and/or adult experiences included traumatically violent events, or secondary, in the sense that their experience of hearing their child recount their experience of traumatic violence has caused them distress and psychological disturbance. Occasionally it is at both levels (see Box 4.3).

Box 4.3: Trauma and post-traumatic stress disorder

Trauma
We can think of psychological trauma as something that creates intense effects of an event on the person, such as: fear, overwhelming stress, lasting shock, dissociation (as a protective action in the moment), and such like.

For further reading in this area, see van der Kolk and McFarlane (1996).

Here is an outline of some of the aspects of post-traumatic stress disorder (PTSD):

- Fear is induced by cues that remind of the traumatic event.
- Hallucinations and flashbacks take the person into an altered state of consciousness in which they may relive the traumatic event.
- Much psychological work is done to suppress memory of the event.
- Dulling of emotion and being 'shut down'.

- Elevated arousal states and distraction behaviour (can be 'kicking off').

- Sleep and attention disturbance.

- Depression and/or suicidal ideas.

For further reading on PTSD, see Brett (1996).

For further reading regarding children and adolescents, see Pynoos, Steinberg and Goenjian (1996).

What to do:

- Identify which issues the person will work with you on.

- Explain the work process.

- Ground talk in the real here and now.

- Where necessary refer to a colleague for eye movement desensitisation and reprocessing (EMDR) or trauma-focused cognitive behavioural therapy (CBT), as these are the two methods in the evidence base and National Institute for Health and Clinical Excellence (NICE) guidelines. The preparatory phases of both involve extended self-soothing techniques and creation of psychological safety.

What not to do:

- Insist on talking about the traumatic events.

- Insist on 'breaking through defences' or the need to re-experience the original pain. These ways of working are known to re-traumatise and actually harm people.

- Allow the person to talk at length without regular use of self-soothing or psychological safety tools. (Think of the more challenging topics such as these like the sun: it's too bright and too painful to look directly for too long; always look away; change the topic as needed.)

- Talk about it to the end of the appointment and then leave. (Always allow the latter two-thirds of an appointment to wind down and de-brief, at least to begin with.)

The standard way of teaching the outline of SLT is to look at what is usually referred to as 'operant conditioning' (Herbert 1978, p.60), which I prefer to call 'learning by consequences'. This involves assessing the 'problem' behaviour in terms of what is holding it in place, as an unintended 'reinforcing consequence', or what will be needed as an intended 'reinforcing consequence' to hold in place the missing, desired behaviour. Often, the simplest way of operationalising this is to use a 'star chart' for rewarding the occurrence of the desired behaviour. The preferred way to deal with unwanted (or 'problem') behaviour is to ignore it. This is called 'extinction' in the more technical literature. This strategy, as with the star chart technique, only works with the simplest of issues, and generally where there is only one identified issue.

Box 4.4: What's simple about SLT

Learning by association
When *this* (stimulus) occurs, *this* behaviour (response) will follow.
When a second stimulus is paired with the first, at the same time, it leads to the same response.
Over time, the second stimulus provokes the same response.
An example is shouting at a child, producing a fear response. When this is done as food is put in front of the child, over time the child becomes fearful when food is presented, and cannot eat it. (This example is from Herbert 1987.)

Learning by consequences

A – Antecedent – what happened before

B – Behaviour – what's in focus

C – Consequence – what happened after

This is based on the idea that something may trigger or initiate a behaviour, but that what happens afterwards is what makes the behaviour more or less likely to recur. This is why we use the terms 'reinforcement' or 'reinforcing consequence'. This is the place where we might add a 'reward' or a token of a reward (a tick or a star on a chart), but a reward is only one of many possible ways of seeing a 'reinforcing consequence'.

Learning by observation and mimicry

This happens for things we want our child to learn and for things we do not want them to learn. This is where seeing adults do 'bad' things, such as hitting or shouting, may show a child how to do them. What happens next is important (back to the A-B-C), as that may mean the behaviour becomes stronger and more stuck.

In the core of this model of human behaviour is the idea that we also learn by trial and error, and that much unwanted/ undesirable behaviour is learnt by mistake. When parents inadvertently pay attention to the unwanted behaviour it also accidentally teaches the child to do it more.

This is where the idea of differential attention comes in:

• Pay more attention to what you want more of.

• Pay less attention to what you want less of.

This is where ignoring the beginnings of unwanted behaviour can be helpful.

Those cases are not the ones referred to children's social care or CAMHS. In even the slightly more complex cases the way of doing these simple techniques is crucial, and a great degree of subtlety and skill is required to perform these well. Given that these are techniques to teach to parents, and given that most of our parents in our children's social care/CAMHS sample are troubled and perhaps, at least secondarily traumatised, there is a great deal to do before using these simple tools. Also, most of our youngsters have multiple issues with their behaviour, may present as if they are oppositional or impulsive and/or have problems of attention. This means that they present much more of a challenge to professionals doing SLT, let alone to parents or carers.

What we need to do with our complex (in Hackney children's social care, the norm) cases is to ensure that we assess carefully at the outset, and review at intervals as we progress. If we can, we should always gather as complete a set of information as possible, not just about the current issues and the family, school and community contexts, but also about the child's history and developmental path, as well as a detailed family history, including the parents' or carers' own childhood and adulthood experiences.

Part of our knowledge gathering, and in many ways the most important, is to observe the family in action. That shows us the patterns of interlocking responses and styles of response, one to another. In referring to 'What's simple about SLT' (Box 4.4), these are the interlocking patterns of Antecedent, Behaviour and Consequence. Often, parents and carers are keen to explain their style of response, and this gives us access to a detailed personal history of the parent or carer. This is an essential component of our assessment, as we need to know the current limits of response and ability for each of the members of the family (see below, regarding Assessment).

Let us now look at some of the ways in which SLT can be applied.

A non-compliant child

This is about as simple a case as we might encounter, outside of a school social work-based service. An eight-year-old boy lives with his mother, who has 'severe and enduring' mental health difficulties. The child has been missing a great deal of school, is not functioning to his ability and is believed to be caught up in his mother's psychotic experiences. The immediate referred issue is how the child can refuse to comply and can become aggressively defiant, when his mother will then back down.

This case was worked on by a parenting support practitioner (PSP) and a children's practitioner (CP) from the social work unit. The core task for the PSP was to help the parent to re-establish useful routines and boundaries, such as sleeping, waking and getting to school. The PSP was able to support the parent directly on the occasions they were in the family home. The core task for the CP was in linking up the many parts of the professional and family networks around the work which the parent was undertaking. This also included helping link up the adult mental health services in a more positive and proactive way, when they had experienced the parent as largely non-compliant.

Our main strategy was to help the parent make appropriate demands in a way which her child could understand and to follow up the beginnings of compliance with encouragement. Similarly, when the child presented undesirable behaviour, such as unreasonable demands or defiance, the parent was encouraged and supported to ignore the first part of these, and immediately to request some other, desirable, behaviour, such as compliance or joining in a practical activity, instead of the undesirable behaviour.

In terms of SLT, this illustrates the 'operant conditioning' model where the Antecedent can be variable (parent inattention or parent request), followed by a target Behaviour of demanding, defiance or opposition, followed by the reinforcing Consequence of the 'goods' demanded or placatory 'goods' being provided by parental compliance. The repaired version involves an Antecedent of parent request, followed by target Behaviour of demanding, defiance or opposition, followed by an absence of reinforcing Consequence (ignoring). The latter component is also quickly followed by a new A-B-C triplet of: Antecedent as parent requests compliance with a different task (one wanted but also maybe more easily achieved), beginnings of desired Behaviour from the child, followed by reinforcing Consequence of parent approval (and possibly a star on a chart, if such is being used).

This case also illustrates the beginnings of a more complex use of SLT. The technique of ignore and immediately invite desired behaviour is called differential reinforcement. The use of this requires a good assessment of parent and child abilities and responsiveness patterns, as well as often split-second timing in the professional, as coach to the parent.

Often we might think of reinforcing consequences as tangible rewards that a child can earn. That can be useful. This strategy is best used for children who may have complex or equivocal relationships with adult carers, and as a way of introducing the influence of parental approval and positive regard alongside the immediately tangible reward object. The really powerful 'reward' is always adult attention and positive regard (maybe in words of praise, but also in the less verbal, performed ways of being with your child), but children who have been groomed for abuse and/or abused are right to be suspicious about adult intentions (see Table 4.1 on p.54).

Box 4.5: What's complex about SLT? The interlocking effects of many dimensions of action

A little bit more theory
Antecedent: the single event or action that takes place before the Behaviour in question (also seen as the Stimulus to Behaviour as Response; see Box 4.4).

Cognitive (also cognition): higher (verbal) level conscious thinking processes leading to (a capacity for) self-reflection and self-command.

Conditioning: a Behaviour is said to be 'conditioned' to a stimulus, or several stimuli (as Antecedent) when the reinforcing Consequence is applied consistently, then intermittently, and the Behaviour is performed regularly.

Consequence (or Reinforcing Consequence): the single event or action that takes place after the Behaviour in question and which makes repetition of the Behaviour more or less likely.

Operant: the voluntary Behaviour that is attached to ('conditioned' to) the Antecedent (as stimulus) by the following reinforcing Consequence (see Box 4.4).

Response: the action, mood or emotional performance that results from the stimulus. Respondent behaviour (the response) is usually seen as 'innate' or involuntary, that is to say, naturally provoked by the stimulus without conscious control or mediation.

Stimulus: the event or action that leads to (provokes) the response.

Time

The most effective interval between Behaviour and Consequence is less than three seconds. This means that speed of intervention is essential.

A-B-Cs are always overlapping, thus:

```
A
B       A
C       B
A       C       etc.
```

This means that intervening with one Consequence may inadvertently trigger another A-B-C chain. Careful assessment and observation is essential.

Differential attention needs even tighter timing. To see the beginnings of unwanted behaviour in one child and to elicit and reinforce wanted behaviour in another means splitting attention between the children with, on occasions, split-second timing.

Severity and complexity

Most of our referred children have multiple behavioural issues and most are quite ingrained habits. These do not simply drop away if ignored.

The more ingrained a habit, the more work is needed to release the child (or adult) from it.

Ignoring needs to be complete; even a glance has to 'see past', not at the behaviour.

Differential reinforcement is to ignore, immediately prompt for wanted behaviour then immediately reinforce the beginnings of the wanted behaviour, all at high speed.

For children who have been exposed to extremes of adult behaviour, amplified versions of praise or approval are needed in order to gain the child's attention and to mark this response as different.

Many of the issues which children are stuck with are ingrained versions of random responses to not knowing what to do: we must always assess fully for missing skills and sequencing abilities, as these may be what provoke the unwanted behaviour in the first place.

'Hidden Antecedents'

The idea of an Antecedent not only means an obvious, outer behaviour by another. It can also mean an inner (I often refer to these as 'hidden') Antecedent, such as a bodily experience with no name, or a 'flashback' of a more obvious kind.

An injured and neglected child

A family of four or five members? This is a common issue for children's social care.

The stepfather had been asked to leave and not visit the household as part of a child protection plan, following allegations that he had caused the injury to the oldest child. The children had been placed in foster care briefly, during the initial phase of assessment, but returned to their mother, following her agreement to the stepfather's exit.

All three children have recently suffered neglect, being poorly and intermittently fed and bathed. The house has been dirty to the point of being a health hazard. The mother of the children has periodic bouts of what would probably be thought of as 'depression', when she takes to her bed for days on end. She does not want to be diagnosed or medicated. She has also on occasions lost her temper and screamed, sworn and shaken or hit the children. The stepfather has been able to rally round on those times, as he has become the mother's partner, so the incidence of neglect and general disorder has been greatly lessened. However, it seems he too would lose his temper with the children.

The children's behavioural difficulties were seen as: oppositional to adult authority (at school as well as at home), frequent fights between the children, general lack of routines and boundaries and 'very demanding'. The oldest girl, who had suffered bruising and lacerations with a sprain, but fortunately no fracture, was seen as the most vocal and most challenging of the three.

At the point of consideration of SLT, there were concerns that the stepfather was in fact at home most of the time.

Following on from the principles of SLT as set out above, we need all adults on board as part of the assessment, let alone the intervention. Similarly, we need to build the maximum possible level of consistency of response both for each parent and between them. It follows therefore that we need both parents to be at home and fully on board with the plan. SLT has been used successfully with injuring parents and their children for some four decades.

Box 4.6: Parent-focused interventions

Kelly (1983) set out a framework for working with parents who had physically abused and injured one or more of their children. This model uses desensitisation, self-soothing and anger management techniques as the foundations, before moving on to deploy specific behavioural techniques. This works well with parents in court proceedings, as well as with parents who are already prepared to change.

Webster-Stratton (2005) has developed the most widely known parenting behaviour training programmes. These are validated for a wide range of populations and issues, particularly for the six- to eight-year-old range. Parents attend a weekly group with other parents and are exposed to video, role-play and discussion. Homework tasks are set. This works with the more organised and compliant families.

Eyberg (see Foote *et al.* 1998) has developed a single-family (often one parent and one child at a time) intensive, clinic-based approach to more stuck and problematic parent or child behaviour. This is conducted weekly, over a set period. It is a good example of the 'three-layer' models, where a worker coaches, cues and rewards with praise the parent (sometimes in the room, sometimes with an in-the-ear device) to do the same with their child. This intensive approach is particularly useful with extreme and long-lasting tantrums (once a child protection assessment clears the way), which otherwise drains and demoralises even the most willing parents.

The first part of the SLT process was to help the professional network engage with the parents around the official return of the stepfather, coupled with engaging both parents in a new plan of action. The second part of the process was to conduct a detailed assessment of the family, focused around the behavioural issues which had been flagged up. This assessment added to the core assessment under way, by gleaning more interactional detail in focused observation and more detail around the parents' and children's patterns of arousal and responsiveness.

Box 4.7: Behavioural assessment

What are each of the people in this situation capable of now?

What is their broad intellectual capacity, as shown in understanding sequences of events and ability to hold in mind a chain of events?

What is their basic disposition? Do they switch rapidly from one state to another and with minimum input from others (their level of biological 'irritability')? When things get tough, what is their 'arousal strategy': do they go 'high' ('hyper-arousal') or 'low' ('hypo-arousal')? Do they switch between these states?

In which situations and with what help can each best focus and stay concentrated on what is going on? How long is a reasonable minimum for each person?

For each behaviour we need to specify it as precisely as possible.

> For each unwanted (aka 'problem') behaviour we need to specify what exactly is wanted in its place. Replacement of unwanted behaviour by wanted behaviour is much more likely to succeed than an attempt at simple 'extinction' (ignoring), particularly with ingrained behaviour.
>
> What are the achievable and realistic rewarding (reinforcing) consequences through which each child will be helped best to hold onto goals?
>
> Chart the frequency, intensity, etc. of the target behaviours over a ten-day period and review in detail.
>
> Target the behaviours in order of achievability more than severity, in order to build up skills and retain motivation.

In the assessment work, we gathered information about the children's birth and life histories, as well as pre-birth information, including the parents' own experiences as children, growing up and as adults. Both parents were able to speak of their own experiences and to give their accounts and explanations of what was happening for them when things went well and when they did not. The stepfather was able to let us know that he had been badly beaten as a child by his mother and when in foster care. The mother was able to tell us that she had large gaps in her memory of her life (see Box 4.3 above, regarding trauma – this is a common experience in a children's social care client group), but that she knew she reacted over and above what her children's behaviour warranted.

With both parents recognising and wanting to work on their arousal patterns, we could then move on to analysing the children's problem behaviours and the missing wanted replacement behaviours in precise detail.

Formulation of the constellation of problem behaviours and missing wanted behaviours included that the oppositional behaviour was managed inconsistently, both in terms of parents' consequential behaviour being inconsistent from time to time and between parents, and in terms of the elevated or depressed level of affect from the parents (from no reaction to screaming and threatening). Aggression by the children was seen as learnt through modelling and then reinforced intermittently by highly affect-laden parental responses, alternating with 'buying off' the problem with sweets or the child being taken out. The core of the planned strategy was to help parents re-motivate, devise practical routines, whereby they could teach the children regular expectations, and to gain energy and hope through small gains in less problematic behaviours, before tackling the main ones through a proactive 'positive parenting' strategy.

For both parents the classic route of desensitisation and relaxation techniques was the beginning point. Once they each had more 'self-mastery' they could take on ideas and practices for helping their children in consistent and safe ways.

Referring to Kelly (1983), the first steps in working with the family are to engage with the parents' and the children's descriptions and explanations of the problem situations. This is a necessary precursor to inviting them in to a behavioural way of thinking and acting. The second step is to analyse in more detail the parents' respective arousal patterns (as in 'When I lose it with the children/my partner'), again, as a precursor to inviting them to work with us to learn new and effective ways of behaving calmly and consistently. The third step is to analyse the range of problem behaviours within specific situations, and to agree a step-wise approach to tackling these in order.

With younger children, no matter how bright and precocious they are, the focus of our work is to allow children to be children, and to encourage parents to parent their children more effectively and peaceably. In this way, any interventions devised with the family are led and managed by the parents, with professionals' support. The key to effective behavioural change is looking for the missing (wanted, pro-social) behaviour which is to replace the over-represented (unwanted, problem) behaviour. This way we use the SLT model most effectively: to promote and reinforce wanted, pro-social behaviour positively and, wherever possible, ignore the unwanted target behaviour, such that the unwanted behaviour dwindles away, while the wanted behaviour grows stronger.

Children in foster care placement

Foster care can be an interesting challenge to the SLT practitioner, as the effectiveness of the foster carers as parent figures can be a feature of the difficulties within the placement. If we consider the core of the SLT model, it tells us that behaviour which is not wanted, but which is still present, is currently being reinforced by some means. Equally, behaviour which is newly appearing in the placement, and which is also not wanted, is being reinforced by some means. In addition to this, the emotional meaning of each foster carer as a 'parent' may be compromised by virtue of one or more of the following: multiple placements of varying lengths, broken promises of permanency, vicarious meeting of adults' emotional needs through caring for the children, marital discord within the foster care couple and carers' birth children taking a quasi-parental role.

Two sisters are in foster care together. This is their eighth placement. They are both of primary school age. The older sister is seen as more challenging, in that she soils, screams and attacks. The younger sister is seen as 'less troubled', as she is compliant at home, but a bully at school, and occasionally seems to invite physical assault of herself. Both seem to be exceptionally bright children, but are under-achieving academically.

The referral is around the possibility that the placement for the older child might end. That poses serious problems for children's social care. Classically the response would be to move the one not 'thriving'. Follow-up research with siblings seems to suggest that separation, even in these circumstances, is detrimental to long-term personal and social adjustment. The narrative accounts of adults brought up in care placements and also separated from their siblings indicate that, while there may be a clear explanation for separation from parents (abuse, neglect, incapacity and so forth) which can help absolve the child from guilt or responsibility, there are no such explanations for separating siblings, and damaging that relationship long term, which do not also blame one or more of the children involved.

One of the parameters of an SLT assessment is the meaning of the behaviour to those involved in its performance. Another parameter is that of appraising the relative 'organism' 'irritability' factors at work alongside the capacity to 'self-soothe' and to master impulses/exercise 'self-mastery'.

The older sister expressed the view that she knew why she did what she did and that she did not like it; indeed she wanted to stop doing it. She also said that there were times when she could stop the 'bad' stuff and do something else. There were also times when that did not work.

Despite this child's young age, and in recognition of her intellectual and self-awareness abilities, part of the overall strategy included CBT elements, as these have a common heritage with SLT, and many of the core practices of CBT are derived from SLT. These elements included the following: specific deep muscle and breathing relaxation techniques; carefully guided visualisation of a safe and healing place; and new cognitions of self-mastery and achievement ('I am...', 'I can...'). These were further reinforced by the foster carers being coached in noticing when the older girl did not do the problem behaviour and instead attempted something else. Great attention and assistance were given to these moments of positive adaptation.

The fruits of this, aside from the placement stabilising, were that more attention could be given to the difficulties with which the younger child was struggling.

A sibling group in adoptive placement

Adoption is an extreme example of the complexity that is involved in influencing children's behaviour, when the parents are relative newcomers into the children's lives. Similarly to foster care, children may arrive in an adoptive placement having had many carers on the way. They may also have experienced broken promises by carers, as well as abuse and/or neglect by their birth family. All in all, it is quite right that children with such experiences should be self-protectively mistrustful of adults and adult authority. Add to this mix that these loving parents have never grown up together in bringing up these children from babies, and are now placed in circumstances that test their couple relationship in new ways.

These particular children had been posted into the future, in the hope that a loving family would help them heal and mend. This is quite typical of the older approaches to adoptive placements. Helpfully, the children rebelled early, when post-adoption support was still readily on tap.

None of the children could sleep properly. Each of the four would take it in turns to start a fight with one or more siblings. The parents dreaded weekends and school holidays.

While the parents both looked outwardly to be relatively calm and consistent with one another, part of what our assessment turned to was to look at the smaller scale of things, the finer nuances of parental behaviour. It is often at this level that things can start to get out of hand. Once the children's behaviour has started to run away with itself, this most often self-amplifies to the point where parental control can only be exercised through drastic and obvious means, such as separating the children into different parts of the house. Obviously, this also serves to reinforce the undesirable behaviour, as each time it takes place the children each get the total attention of at least one parent. As we saw above, it is relationship rewards, such as the full attention of a parent, which ultimately are the strongest.

One of the things we did was to use detailed observation. It is often best to use this at the time which the family see as most challenging, or most often going awry. In this case it was the early evening meal time. In reviewing the record with the parents, we could pick out their different observations of events and their different interpretations of interactional moments. This helped the parents use each other's different awareness to build a stronger and more cohesive consistency of parenting behaviour. In addition, by focusing on the moments before things started to run away, it gave the parents the opportunity to load the children's desirable behaviour with parental attention, and over time to help the children do more of what was wanted and less of what was not helpful.

On the back of this, we were able to introduce some family sessions of 'self-soothing' skills, so that everyone could relax and experience safety and calmness together, prior to bedtime. Quite often, the 'hyper-arousal' or hyper-alertness of children is, as it were, programmed in from early experiences of danger, to the extent that this becomes a normal bodily state. Over time, this will diminish, as alternative bodily states can be reinforced and supported instead.

Box 4.8: Intervention fit

Has the reduction in the unwanted (target 1) behaviour held up since beginning the intervention?

Is the replacement 1 behaviour beginning to take hold?

If yes, then:

- Introduce target 2 and its replacement 2 as an overlapping schedule of reinforcement.

- Let the reinforcement of replacement 1 become intermittent, as the behaviour is more reliably present, and fade out entirely when on to the second overlap (target 3 and replacement 3). Repeat.

If no, then:

- Re-assess for other reinforcing consequences, holding target behaviour 1 in place, including parent or child arousal states; re-assess for inconsistencies or interruptions to the reinforcement of replacement 1. Conduct another baseline measurement, then proceed as before. Repeat the self-soothing training and homework if necessary (check that they can do it by asking the family to show how they do it).

Table 4.1 When to use SLT and when not to use SLT

Examples of when to use SLT	Examples of when not to use SLT
Parents **Deficits** Lack of care and caring routines Lack of positive modelling of behaviour Lack of positive responses to children's 'good' behaviour **Surpluses** Parent shouting at/arguing with child (note: screen for domestic violence) Parent hitting or injuring child (see above) **Children/young people** **Deficits** Lack of specific practical or self-care skills Lack of required behaviour Poor attention/concentration/attainment Lack of cooperative behaviour **Surpluses** Oppositional behaviour Defiant behaviour Aggression Tantrums Most children and adolescents' emotional and behavioural difficulties Many mental health difficulties, for example phobias of school and other things, as well as diagnosed behavioural difficulties under various terms	When there are allegations of grooming of children for sexual abuse When a 'Schedule 1 Offender' is part of the social network of the parents, but this is denied or minimised When no adult will accept responsibility for physical injury, even as an 'accident' When strangers (as in unnamed adults) are allowed into the house and no complete social data is available SLT is possible in most other circumstances; however, the key to success is a careful assessment of the whole family Where parents or carers show signs of hyper-arousal and possibly signs of trauma, then these need to be identified and worked with first

A kind of conclusion

One of the key features of the cases described above is that the bulk of the work encounters did and should take place in the family home, not in an office or clinic setting. While the mental health feature of the issues may seem strongly apparent (although not medicalised or described in technical detail herein), we must bear in mind that these are ordinary, for children's social work/social care staff, 'bread and butter' cases. The difficulties and the suffering of the family members are real and apparent, and they have a right to skilled social work interventions, and clinical interventions where needed.

All too often, social workers have been taught not to try to work, but to refer on to the 'experts' in tier 3 CAMHS. It is rare that tier 3 CAMHS staff are allowed to do much work outside of their clinic base. Given that the above cases benefit most from work within their natural environment, it has all too often been the case that these cases fall between the two stools of children's social work and CAMHS. I hope that I have shown that the SLT skill set can enable the willing practitioner to undertake work in the family home (and school, where we can), and be of real and lasting help to families of all configurations who need it.

With a minimum of an introductory course and skilled consultation, all staff practising directly with children and their families can take SLT out to the vast majority of families for whom SLT will be of help.

References

Andersen, T. (1996) 'Language is not Innocent.' In F. Kaslow (ed.) *Handbook of Relational Diagnosis*. Chichester: Wiley.

Bandura, A. (1977) *Social Learning Theory*. Upper Saddle River, NJ: Prentice Hall.

Brett, E. (1996) 'Classification of Posttraumatic Stress Disorder.' In B. van der Kolk, A. McFarlane and L. Weisaeth (eds) *Traumatic Stress*. London: Guilford Press.

Foote, R., Schumann, E., Jones, M. and Eyberg, S. (1998) 'Parent-child interaction therapy: a guide for clinicians.' *Clinical Child Psychology and Psychiatry 3*, 3, 361–373.

Gelles, R.J. and Cornell, C.P. (1990) *Intimate Violence in Families*. London: Sage Publications.

Hazen, A.L., Connelly, C.D., Kelleher, K., Landsverk, J. and Barth, R. (2004) 'Intimate partner violence among female caregivers of children reported for child maltreatment.' *Child Abuse & Neglect 28*, 3, 301–319.

Herbert, M. (1978) *Conduct Disorders of Childhood and Adolescence*. Chichester: Wiley.

Herbert, M. (1987) *Behavioural Treatment of Children with Problems* (2nd Edition). London: Academic Press.

Higgins, G. (1994) 'Children's Accounts.' In A. Mullender and R. Morley (eds) *Children Living with Domestic Violence.* London: Whiting & Birch.

Hyden, M. and McCarthy, I.C. (1994) 'Woman battering and father–daughter incest disclosure: discourses of denial and acknowledgement.' *Discourse and Society 5,* 4, 543–565.

Kelleher, K., Hazen, A.L., Coben, J.H., Wang, Y. *et al.* (2008) 'Self-reported disciplinary practices among women in the child welfare system.' *Child Abuse and Neglect 32,* 8, 811–818.

Kelly, J. (1983) *Treating Child-Abusive Families.* London: Plenum Press.

Kempe, C.H. and Helfer, R.E. (eds) (1968) *The Battered Child.* Chicago, IL: Chicago University Press.

Mayor of London (2005) *The London Domestic Violence Strategy.* London: Greater London Assembly.

Moore, D.R. and Florsheim, P. (2008) 'Interpartner conflict and child abuse risk among African American and Latino adolescent parenting couples.' *Child Abuse and Neglect 32,* 4, 463–475.

Mullender, A., Hague, G., Imam, U., Kelly, L., Malos, E. and Regan, L. (2002) *Children's Perspectives on Domestic Violence.* London: Sage Publications.

Pynoos, R., Steinberg, A. and Goenjian, A. (1996) 'Traumatic Stress in Childhood and Adolescence.' In B. van der Kolk, A. McFarlane and L. Weisaeth (eds) *Traumatic Stress.* London: Guilford Press.

van der Kolk, B. and McFarlane, A. (1996) 'The Black Hole of Trauma.' In B. van der Kolk, A. McFarlane and L. Weisaeth (eds) *Traumatic Stress.* London: Guilford Press.

van der Kolk, B., McFarlane, A. and Weisaeth, L. (eds) (1996) *Traumatic Stress.* London: Guilford Press.

Webster-Stratton, C. (2005) *The Incredible Years* (Revised Edition). Seattle, WA: Incredible Years.

Webster-Stratton, C. and Herbert, M. (1994) *Troubled Families – Problem Children.* Chichester: Wiley.

CHAPTER 5

Stories Lived, Stories Told

Using a Systemic Approach to Case Recording in the Social Work Unit

Julie Rooke

When our social work unit began working with the Jackson family, they had accumulated more than seven volumes of social care files. Perhaps more – files are, in my experience, notoriously hard to track down from mysterious archive locations. Each file was full of description – pieces of written information, including assessments, statements, write-ups of visits, supervision records – that considered together, gave a hazy description of a mother with two children and a lot of problems. The files told a story – a problem-saturated, disjointed tale – of a family with multiple generations of problems and social care involvement. As a consultant social worker in the Children in Need (CIN) service, I was to lead my social work unit through work with this family in the hope of creating change for them.

In this chapter I explore how recorded information shapes our understanding of problems, and how thinking and recording systemically may help us to think differently about the problems families face. Recording is an integral part of the interventions we carry out in social care, but we think too about its impact – on us, on future workers and on the children and families themselves. I consider in this chapter the relationship between our interventions and recording, and how working within the systemic and behavioural approach of Reclaiming Social Work has shaped this relationship.

Annie Jackson was a teenager when her stepfather began sexually abusing her. By the time her second child Joanne was born (who is now seven), Annie had acquired a dependency on alcohol, diagnoses of personality disorder and depression, and multiple experiences of domestic violence. Joanne and her brother Daniel, now aged 11, had witnessed their mother passed out from drink multiple times, spent periods of time in foster care and had the police visit the home numerous times after fights between their parents. Daniel was withdrawing and missing weeks of school at a time. Joanne was acting out at school and at home. They were known to our unit as children in need, having previously been subject to child protection plans. They were, in social care language, at risk of emotional abuse and neglect. They were living out a story that had chapters spanning generations, and reading the files gave one a sense of some hopelessness – could anything be different?

Words on the written page are powerful. They are, in many ways, immortal – they outlive the circumstances in which they are written, and often the authors that penned them. In a system notorious for high worker turnover, the words of those who went before are heavily relied on to carry on the required tasks. Words shape the truth of what comes next. Social constructionism posits that language shapes, and indeed defines, 'truth' – which is in fact not fixed or absolute, but is historically and culturally defined (Burr 1995). Words mean nothing in isolation, but together they relay meaning, and the words we choose don't just describe a situation; they give it meaning. Narrative therapists suggest that a 'problem-saturated story limits perspective, edits our threads of hope and positive meaning, and precludes refreshing possibilities and potentials. Change may then seem impossible...' (Freeman, Epston and Labovits 1997, p.48). When encountered with a problem-saturated story in a social care case file, does reading it preclude potential? Does change seem impossible – both to the professionals working with the family and to the family members themselves?

Why do we record what we do? For whom are we recording this information – these stories? And how do we do it? These are just some of the interesting questions that as a social work unit we began asking ourselves. Far from simply proving to managers that we were doing our work, we began to consider recording as part of the interventions we were providing for our families – and the powerful effect that changing the process by which we record information might have on us, other practitioners and, importantly, families, now and in the future. Inspired by the ideas of solution-focused and narrative therapy, and using a social constructionist lens, we started to think more consciously of recording as story-making. But with this new thinking came new questions… Who writes the story? Whose language do we write it in? And does the way the story is written influence the way the story is lived out?

In the social work unit we are taking a fresh approach to the way we work with children and families, and this includes the way we record our interventions. In a traditional social work team, an individual social worker working with a family usually meets monthly with a team manager for supervision, and the record of the discussion that takes place about a family would probably look something like a 'to-do list'. In the case of the Jackson family, it might look something like this:

1. Refer Mrs Jackson to alcohol counselling.

2. Contact education welfare officer re: Daniel's non-attendance.

3. Explore respite care possibilities within the family network and discuss options with Mrs Jackson.

4. Refer Joanne to education psychologist at school.

These lists are not without their uses – they give social workers, particularly those newly qualified or without experience in child protection, a clear outline of the work that has been agreed with the team manager. They provide a way for managers to track the progress of cases (and the work being undertaken by social workers), thereby providing a means of accountability. They are pretty easy, if uninteresting, to read. What these lists don't do is reflect any of the complexity of the situations that families in our service find themselves in – something which may well make up part of the discussion within supervision but is, in my experience, less frequently documented or reflected in written records. A write-up like this doesn't reflect the richness of critical thinking that needs to take place when considering some of the most complex and difficult cases that we deal with.

In contrast, in the social work unit we meet every week to discuss each child we are working with. Taking the place of monthly supervision (which does take place, but is reserved for individual reflection and career development, rather than case management), unit meetings are a live, dynamic, current meeting-of-the-minds of five professionals working closely with the same families. The essence of these discussions is recorded by the unit coordinator, highlighting the need for competent, interested and engaged professionals with administrative skills. These minutes then form part of the child's social care record. With a record of discussion being added each week, a narrative begins to emerge, and the reader sees not just a series of stand-alone documents, or an ever growing to-do list, but a moving, flowing analysis which goes some way in reflecting the complexity and ever-changing realities of the children we work with. Decisions are documented (and the thinking that informed these decisions), but so too are changes in thinking, alternative observations, and most importantly, changes in direction with the addition of new information. Part of a unit meeting discussion about the Jackson family might be recorded something like this:

> The unit discussed the current difficulties that Daniel is experiencing. We all agreed that we are worried that Daniel is at risk of being excluded from school. Being home with Annie for most of the day also increases the risk of physical altercations between them, which have happened in the past, thus increasing the risk of harm to Daniel. We have observed that Annie is more likely to report drinking during these times. Annie has told the consultant social worker that she believes Daniel is being bullied at school, but the children's practitioner, informed by his direct work with Daniel, thinks he might be staying home to look after his mum.
>
> *Actions agreed:* the children's practitioner will meet with the education welfare officer to talk about strategies to encourage Daniel to go to school, while acknowledging his worries about his mum. Family therapist to meet with Daniel and Annie together next week to explore further areas of agreement/disagreement between Daniel and Annie about school. Consultant social worker to meet with Annie to talk about her current drinking and explore possibilities for treatment.

When we began in our social work unit, we wanted to ensure that our discussions were recorded to reflect the thinking we were doing. In the above example, the reader gets the sense that the unit is thinking about these children within the context of their wider surroundings. The reader will also see that different unit members may, as a result of their engagement with different members of the family system, have different hypotheses about what is going on for the family, and that it is only in discussing these together as a unit (a parallel system) that the richness of systemic thinking comes alive. It also demonstrates that the assessments and interventions being carried out with this family are contributed to by the whole unit.

The unit discussion record doesn't have to be wordy. In fact, there is something to be said about being concise, and not repeating information that doesn't need to be reiterated. Apart from the ideological changes we were experiencing in the social work unit, there was a very pragmatic advantage to the weekly unit meeting discussion – there was always evidence on the file of the work that was being undertaken. Even if individual visit write-ups were late being placed on the file, there was evidence of work, or reasons documented why something hadn't been completed. And because the unit meeting discussion was a free-form document (no tick boxes!), we had the freedom to ensure that what we were documenting was congruous with what we were doing.

We were doing things differently. It felt good, and it made sense to us. But does this new way of recording have any impact on families? My hypothesis is that a more richly and thought-inspired written narrative may help families themselves (along with the professionals who help them) shift some of those problem-saturated stories. Far from being a collection of words collecting dust in the archives, I think that the way we record families' experiences may directly affect the way our families live out their stories. Narrative therapists talk about thickening an alternative story in order to help people start to live out those new ways of being (Morgan 2000). Could the same be said about social care records?

Alternative stories do not imply omitting negative attributes. As part of the complex task of managing risk to children, it is imperative that we clearly identify those risks and know when there are no longer enough protective factors for children to remain safely where they are. An alternative story, and a critical reflection of a family's situation, absolutely must reflect the analysis of risk by professionals. But what that means is that it is a balanced and accurate narrative, one which when read, goes somewhere to explain to the reader (including families) why the professionals have come to the decisions they have, even if these include a very difficult decision such as seeking an order to remove a child from their home. I strongly believe that even these decisions can be documented and thought out in a rich, full way, and that the stories that accompany these actions can be influential on the children and parents involved after the fact. It must be infinitely easier (while still the most difficult of tasks) to read a thought-out, balanced story about the removal of your child than simply 'Seek EPO [Emergency Protection Order] because of risk of harm.' I strongly believe that reading (or hearing) a thought-out, balanced, respectful account of actions such as the decision to remove a child from their family may help a family think about that decision differently, and help them to carry on in their lives with a story that is respectful and more likely resonant with them.

Within the social work unit, we have the space and opportunity to consider these difficult decisions and how to articulate these to families in a way that makes most sense to them, rather than the way we may have always done it in the past, no matter who the family. We have the flexibility to choose the professional best placed to deliver information and explain it to a particular family. Pertinently we have the opportunity to reflect on these decisions together, allowing us to consider how we might do things similarly or differently in future, acknowledging the emotional content of what we are doing and respecting the hugely complex and challenging work that we are engaging in with families. The richness of this reflection is documented in the unit meeting discussion, and should be evident to those who come later to find out why and how a decision or action was taken.

When we first started to work with the Jacksons, Annie urged me to read all the backfiles on her family. It was an interesting request; previously I might have thought that families gave little or no consideration to what was recorded about them. But of course for a family like the Jacksons, who for more than a generation have been telling and re-telling their stories to social worker after social worker, they are keenly aware that what is written about them has a powerful effect on the conclusions that the professionals in front of them will draw – even before a first meeting. Frequent worker turnover and high caseloads mean that we rely even more heavily on records to inform our thinking about families right from the beginning. But families tire of telling and re-telling their stories. Imagine how draining it must be to have to re-tell that problem-saturated story over a hundred times, each time having to step back into it and live in it for that moment. No wonder Annie wanted me to read it all rather than face re-telling me her story.

Annie had seen her social care records, and some of those held on her children. She had read child protection reports and assessments written by psychiatrists. She knew the language of risk and problems. She was becoming proficient in the language contained within those reports – as were, worryingly, her children. They were living the problem-saturated stories that had been weaved over time, and it was hard to recognise that anything different might be happening in their lives now. Annie struggled to identify what was going right for her and her children. Somehow the language of problems had become more accessible to them, and in my view, this was having the effect of reinforcing those negative experiences within the family. The talk in the home was negative, so pretty soon everything in the home seemed negative.

Reading those files gives a picture of a family that has struggled for a long time to manage. Right away my first question was, what do we do? Everything's been tried! But what in those records was giving me that impression? I believe that the language of problems influences the meanings that we attribute to situations as practitioners. We are starting to record differently now. Will that mean that future practitioners will read back on these records and attribute different meanings to a family's situation when they come to the attention of services, possibly in another generation? Will the way we record have a possible effect on the interventions of the future with the family? It is my hope that working systemically, and recording systemically, will influence the way future workers understand the problems of these families, no matter how 'entrenched' we believe those problems to be.

As with anything new, there are always challenges. I have already mentioned the reliance on the unit coordinator to be skilled, informed and able to record accurately and succinctly a complex discussion that sometimes lasts 30 minutes. This is a tall order for anyone, and a challenge for any organisation to recruit enough skilled, able staff with administrative skills. The quality of the records comes down to the skill within the unit, and as a consultant social worker, I spent a lot of time reviewing and editing the record of discussions. Of course there are problems inherent to that – I found myself sometimes editing the record not because it needed to be changed but because I thought there was another way of saying something that, to my ear, read better. Somehow in that process, I might have been changing those records from a collective account to one that suited my agenda, and reflected my own language. Was I putting my own stamp too much on these records? I was balancing my responsibilities as overall case holder with my obligation to be true to a multi-professional model of working. This is a difficult balance to achieve in so many ways, and definitely extends to the way we document our work.

Apart from the challenge of documenting a rich and thorough discussion, there is also the challenging task of balancing multiple voices, from multiple professions. Do you think that five people in social care speak the same way, with the same language? Think again! This is the beauty of the unit model, but the challenge as well. At the end of a discussion, we needed to come to a consensus about what to do – at least temporarily – and sometimes this meant one person taking the final view. This is the role of the consultant social worker. I decided what was in and what was out, both within the meeting, and following, in my editing of the records before they were placed on the file. So are the records more a reflection of the consultant social worker's thinking? Do they actually reflect the thinking, at times contrary, of five professional points of view? Or do they gloss over this, and give a more definitive view than is the reality? The competing purposes of accountability and multi-professional thinking are always present, and that balance is sometimes difficult to achieve.

An important part of working together with families is sharing written information that we write about them. The challenge to this are documents which display information poorly or inaccurately, making it difficult for families (and other professionals) to understand what information has been gathered and what conclusions have been reached. For example, a core assessment with numerous tick boxes and copious pages is not only disheartening to write; it must be equally disheartening and difficult to read and make sense of. Forms that are too prescriptive don't allow practitioners to articulate information in a way that makes it clear how they have come to the conclusions they have, and in my experience families are not likely to read through those types of records with any sense that the information contained within them relates to them. By contrast, working in a systemic way and ensuring the ability to have free-form recording wherever possible allows practitioners to tailor records to the unique aspects of a family.

For a long time it has been posited that record keeping is not just as an administrative task, but part of the intervention itself with a family. Given this, how should we approach the task differently? Currently, record keeping is seen as a time-consuming, onerous task, even within the social work unit model. If we start to change our thinking about the usefulness for children and families of the recording process away from a simple administrative and management function to one of intervention, I believe that we would become even more effective and thoughtful in the records we keep. How would we do things differently if families regularly viewed the unit meeting discussion records? If we invited parents and children to write their own comments and additions in these notes? Far from disagreeing with everything we said, I suspect that we would find some consensus with families about the struggles and strengths in their lives, and in the meantime, we would be doing something hugely empowering and enabling for them. We would be inviting families to re-story their lives with us.

During our work with the Jacksons, we endeavoured to put into practice these ideas about re-storying and working together to create change. It was challenging work, and change in families with entrenched problems can be slow. One heartening outcome of our work was the difference that Annie and her children noticed about what we were doing – despite years of services, they could see that we were doing things differently, and that in itself gave them hope that things could change for them too. Annie noted how the children noticed that people came to see them, and not just their mum. Annie felt part of the goals we were setting and was glad that she could always get someone on the telephone who knew who she was. And Annie, who had often resisted assistance such as more childcare or respite support, was able to consider these options, because, as she said, she felt part of the decision, and felt that this was presented to her in a way that was clear, respectful and didn't make her feel embarrassed.

Language is key to thinking and understanding systemically. Language can bring to life the complexity of problems experienced by families like the Jacksons. In the social work units, record keeping has come out of the archives, had the dust blown off it, and is taking centre stage in the way we work. It is my hope that families like the Jacksons will benefit now and in the future from practitioners who are more conscious of the words they use, and the power of narrative in helping families to live their lives more positively.

Commentary by Yvonne Shemmings and David Shemmings

We were immediately struck by the powerful first sentence: 'When our social work unit began working with the Jackson family, they had accumulated more than seven volumes of social care files.' The equally important point is made that there are 'Perhaps more – files are, in my experience, notoriously hard to track down from mysterious archive locations.' With a facility for evocative language [the author] concludes the first paragraph by reminding us that the 'The files told a story – a problem-saturated, disjointed tale – of a family with multiple generations of problems and social care involvement', and encourages practitioners to be vigilant when compiling records, reports and files.

One of us (Yvonne) undertook some of the early pioneering research into the sharing of records and it is reassuring to see that this notion features strongly in this chapter (Raymond 1986). But having now worked with over 8000 professionals on improving their recording, we are aware of a problem when participants hear about 'sharing records': they often assume that they should refrain from saying anything critical or that the family members don't agree with. The danger is that practitioners either write bland, overly descriptive records, which 'say' very little – 'I visited Mrs Green last Friday, and all seemed fine' – or the file becomes too 'clean', devoid of any entries that might be perceived as drawing attention to problems with, for example, a parent's sensitivity towards one or more of their children.

It is worth remembering that a good record is precisely that: a record of *that which has already been communicated* to the parent verbally. In most circumstances there shouldn't be anything new or surprising in the files, or stated at a meeting about the child or family. So in answer to the questions 'Who writes the story?' 'Whose language do we write it in?' we believe the right response in child protection work is, respectively, *the practitioner/'s…*but they should be consulting fully with family members because any disagreements and misunderstandings need to be corrected and clarified in detail with them. It is disingenuous, though, to suggest that recording could be completed as part of a negotiated approach. To guarantee a collaborative enterprise, with the promise of bargaining over words and assessments, is a mistake.

We have noticed a tendency among some social workers to resist or be wary of the notion that they should 'own' their assessments by stating clearly that this is 'my' professional judgement, my viewpoint, given what I've seen, etc. This may reflect a simple lack of confidence or it may betray a preference for an unhelpfully relativistic post-modern confusion about the nature of 'truth'. As the British philosopher Mary Midgley puts it in her autobiographical memoir *The Owl of Minerva*:

> It does not mean that we cannot know anything until we know everything. Human cultures contain all sorts of convenient ways

of breaking the world into manageable handfuls and dealing with one part at a time… Attending to the background pattern of questions and answers does not tip us into a helpless relativism. (Midgley 2005, p.72)

We think social workers shouldn't worry too excessively about '…putting my own stamp too much on these records'. We would prefer to see more practitioners confidently owning their records, provided they have checked them out with family members without sanitising them in the process. It doesn't follow that a confident social worker is disempowering service users. But this inevitably means that, as they develop experience and 'practice wisdom', practitioners need to develop the confidence to be able to say 'difficult things while cuddling the family member but without the cuddle getting in the way of the difficult things that need saying'. A mother used this phrase when one of us (David) undertook research into parents' views of attending child protection throughout (Shemmings and Shemmings 1996, p.70). She was asked to define the attributes of a 'good social worker' and she was one of many to highlight the important balance that constantly has to be struck between, on the one hand, openness, transparency and honesty and, on the other, the raising of concerns when investigating child protection allegations. (This research was also conducted in Hackney, at that time the UK pioneer of family participation in child protection processes.)

The challenge for social workers was summarised well (if a little brutally!) by the other key researcher at the time on user participation, John Øvretveit. After studying social work records, he concluded pithily that while a competent social worker could write a 'bad' record, a less than competent social worker could not write a good one (Øvretveit 1986)! Perhaps that's a little harsh, but we think he made an important point.

Also alluded to is the implication that the record needs to contain a 'golden thread' of continuity over time; otherwise, if each new worker ignores the past by automatically donning new lenses through which to view the family, there is a danger of unwittingly falling prey to what Marian Brandon referred to as the 'start again syndrome' (Brandon et al. 2009): assessing the present and predicting the future without reference to the past. As this chapter powerfully states, 'words shape the truth of what comes next'; but we must always be open to the possibility that the words are accurate. If it is correct that 'Annie Jackson was a teenager when her stepfather began sexually abusing her', then it must be available in the file for future workers who will not always remember (or even know) that this happened.

We were pleased to see the inference made that information needs to be analysed. We have made the point over the years that social workers have become extremely proficient at information *gathering*...but they more often than not leave it *under-analysed*. Jonathan Dickens' research extends this observation. He found that judges, magistrates and lawyers thought that, generally speaking, social workers did not argue their 'case' (that is, their 'position') very well. They relied too heavily on the presentation of 'facts' rather than addressing the more important task of showing how and why the information gathered indicated abuse, neglect and concern (Dickens 2005). Simply reiterating the information gathered is not enough and, in that form, a competent barrister will make mincemeat of the unsuspecting social worker.

References

Burr, V. (1995) 'What is Social Constructionism?' In K. Gergen (ed.) *An Introduction to Social Constructionism.* New York: Routledge.

Brandon, M., Bailey, S., Belderson, P., Warren, C., Gardner, R. and Dodsworth, J. (2009) *Understanding Serious Case Reviews and Their Impact.* London: Department for Children, Schools and Families.

Dickens, J. (2005) 'Being "the epitome of reason": The challenges for lawyers and social workers in child care proceedings.' *International Journal of Law, Policy and the Family* *19*, 1, 73–101.

Freeman, J., Epston, D. and Lobovits, D. (1997) *Playful Approaches to Serious Problems.* New York: Norton Press.

Midgley, M. (2005) *The Owl of Minerva: A Memoir.* London: Routledge.

Morgan, A. (2000) *What Is Narrative Therapy? An Easy-to-Read Introduction.* Adelaide: Dulwich Centre Publications.

Øvretveit, J. (1986) *Improving Social Work Records and Practice.* Birmingham: BASW.

Raymond, Y. (1986) 'Empowerment in practice: Clients' views to seeing records.' *Practice*, Spring, 5–23.

Shemmings, D. and Shemmings, Y. (1996) 'Building Trust when Making Enquiries'. In D. Shemmings and D. Platt (eds) *Making Enquiries into Alleged Child Abuse and Neglect.* Chichester: Wiley.

CHAPTER 6

Preconditions
Structure, Continuity and Momentum

Karen Schiltroth

Why talk about structure?

No doubt, much of this book will be about relationships, narratives, co-construction, finding new solutions, re-writing old stories. And so it should be. This was always the hope of Reclaiming Social Work, that systemic thinking and action would begin to find its way into the work on a day-to-day basis rather than something you referred out for.

But why Reclaiming Social Work, why all the structural changes? What is it about Reclaiming Social Work that makes space for a more therapeutic approach to the work? Wouldn't it be simpler to embed systemic training in social work training and leave teams and workers the way they are? Can't any system support a relationship with good practice from social workers and good clinical supervision?

While social work has always articulated that developing relationships is its professional strength, the child protection system in particular hasn't always been able to achieve this fundamental starting block. Where the current line management and case allocation system has struggled to provide the continuity necessary for effective intervention, Reclaiming Social Work is making real progress. Staff turnover is down, vacancies are almost non-existent and there is a much reduced reliance on agency staff (Cross, Hubbard and Munro 2010), all of which increase our chances of providing a continuous working relationship. What makes Reclaiming Social Work so good at building relationships? Why are the same skilled practitioners, who have come from other systems, having more success with their relationships in 'this' system? Weren't we skilled, well meaning, motivated and hard working social workers before we got here?

Of course we were. But I doubt that systemic training would have made a substantial difference to my individual practice before Reclaiming Social Work. So, I think there is something more happening than the ideas and the language and the approach. The structure of the unit, for me, has been essential in enabling a different kind of relationship.

Reclaiming Social Work is ambitious in its attempt to be more systemic and to utilise more evidence-based interventions, not only because these are difficult things to achieve but because the local authority is not tasked with or rewarded for doing these things. It is tasked with and evaluated on its timely completion of processes (assessments, investigations, reviews), busyness (frequency of visits) and throughput of cases (time subject of a Child Protection Plan).

Statutory social work, regardless of how systemic, therapeutic or constructivist it aims to be, will always be statutory. We work in a highly regularised and proceduralised environment that is subject to intense, authoritarian and unforgiving scrutiny – by family courts and the media. Few therapeutic contexts work with the same kind of oversight and when they do (forensic mental health, for example), they are not renowned for being 'progressive', 'empowering' or 'supportive' to the end user, although the term 'draconian' does come up from time to time.

The task of systemically informed practice, then, is to *manage the bureaucracy* effectively in a way that meets targets and regulatory functions without disturbing the *real* work – relationship building, co-constructing problems and enabling change through strengths-based approaches.

Structure as a systemic construct

If we think of cybernetics, the social work unit sits around the family as it moves through the larger child protection system. This internal system acts as both a buffer against system changes (such as staff turnover) and institutional power, but also mobilises resources in the face of institutional inertia. The effective management of these system issues addresses what I believe have been major inhibitors to building a therapeutic alliance with families in the child protection system. I now look at each of these ideas separately.

Institutional inertia: the little engine that could

The social work unit is a small sub-system within a large web of systems designed to support families; navigating Inland Revenue, housing departments, school admissions and immigration is very difficult for families whose circumstances fall outside the norm, however. The unit is structured to manoeuvre both internal and external financial and information systems reliably and efficiently. For families with multiple problems, cumulative stressors have a huge impact on parenting. Solving problems relating to finance, housing and immigration, or organising payments for play schemes or winter clothing are important, and crucially, many are within our control.

A social work unit gets the forms filled, signed, delivered and transformed into services – day nursery, summer schemes, bedding, short breaks, trainers and a winter coat, moving van or a taxi for hospital appointments. We get benefits transferred, housing arrears waived, immigration decisions appealed and injunctions ordered. We make the boundaries to other organisations and services permeable. This doesn't sound novel; social workers have always done these tasks. The difference in Reclaiming Social Work is that social workers don't do these tasks, unit coordinators do, and they do it fast. Really fast.

Certainly, social workers will identify the need with the family, draft the report, sign on the dotted line, but it is the unit coordinators who do the hard work and make these things happen. They sit on hold with the Home Office and re-send the forms which get lost, chase solicitors for replies and chase us for replies. They're the ones who keep things moving. In the old system, social workers would play phone tag with solicitors, benefit advisers and service providers for days if not weeks. Unit coordinators complete tasks within a couple of days, if not the same day.

But what's really interesting about this is that families understand this role and make effective use of it. They won't spend three days playing phone tag with me. They know that I'll set the wheels in motion but it's the unit coordinator, Sophie, who delivers. They'll ring her with the missing bank details or Nan's address or to say that Jamal is too sick for contact with his mother today. And they love that someone knows what they're talking about and what to do with the information. They love that we were expecting their call. And we love that they call.

It's rather obvious that this unit coordinator role frees up social workers for the task of relationship building, but getting these things done is a crucial aspect of relationship building itself. We so often ask families what they have done, but it is equally important that we deliver on our promises as well.

Continuity: being known versus being understood

Staff turnover in children's services in London authorities is high, although less so in Hackney these days. But inevitably, people come and go. They get sick, take holidays, get promoted, have children and go travelling. They end their relationship with clients. One change in social worker may be tolerable, two frustrating, more than two, well, it's possible that now the system is creating a pattern of unreliability and mistrust that even a well functioning family with interest in an intervention would be unwilling to persevere with.

The unit comprises five people, all with different roles. The consultant social worker and social worker focus on risk assessment, planning and intervention; children's practitioners are tasked with keeping children's experiences in the front of our minds through their relationship and understanding of children's experiences; clinicians bring a systemic view, slowing us down and keeping us curious about possible explanations and ways forward; and unit coordinators provide crucial business support. But all have a good grasp of the family; we know more than the work being done, we understand the key relationships, risks and strengths, important events and subtle patterns. If someone leaves the unit, for a week-long holiday or for good, the family need not begin again. There are other relationships which persist. Family members are familiar with different people in the unit and know that if one is unavailable, another is able to address their immediate concerns. The unit is a small place within a large system to which families have reliable access, where they feel understood and important. It provides a degree of stability and availability that a single individual cannot.

I think one of our defining moments as a unit was when a parent's call was answered by the only unit member to whom she had not yet spoken on the phone.

> Are you from my cluster? I don't recognise your voice. I want to speak to someone from my cluster.

Simonne, our children's practitioner, reassured her that she was from the 'cluster' and knew all about trying to get the benefits transferred (to shift a balance of power within an abusive marital relationship), and she knew that Sophie had confirmed the transfer this morning and gave her the expected payment date. The parent was thrilled, and asked when Simonne would be visiting as they hadn't met yet. And that was it, a cluster was born.

I have reflected on this moment often. Why is it so important to speak to someone from the cluster? Not a manager, not someone to complain to. Just someone, anyone, from the cluster. When you work alone, you work alone. You have your cases, see a manager once a month for supervision and when you're not in, your families are at the mercy of the duty office. Thinking of the example above, in the absence of her allocated worker a parent might be able to muster to the duty worker 'Can you let me know if my benefits will be transferred today?' It is much less likely she would provide this by way of explanation:

> I need to know today if I'll have the money before Friday. Friday is the Sabbath; on Thursday I am supposed to go grocery shopping with my neighbour. This is an appropriate time for me to spend with my support network and has been negotiated with my husband. He will not give me enough money; I need access to my own.

The response to the former is, 'Your social worker will ring when she's back on Monday.' Your response to the detailed request might be better, if you could just get it out. Or, it might not matter even if you could spell it out because there is no one else who can prioritise this, who understands its relevance for this family. There will always be an important narrative about what seems like an insignificant task that a family has enquired about. If it wasn't significant, they wouldn't be ringing.

The difference between being 'known' and being 'understood' becomes more salient when we think about crisis points in the family. And in this context, the unit's capacity to understand the family, even in the absence of a keyworker, is crucial to managing the tension between the investigation and scrutiny functions of the local authority and its duty to effect change by working in partnership.

The client's experience of the unit as accessible and reliable creates a context where they are more likely to trust us, more likely to be available to us and importantly, more likely to take risks which lead to change.

Continuity during investigation: hanging on to the big picture while moving through acute crisis

Child protection services exercise some of the most acute forms of social control. Investigative responsibilities are often experienced by families as disempowering and traumatic.

When you work in isolation, you are often the only person with a good understanding of the progress a family is making. While your manager may have an overview of the key risks and planned work, it is unlikely they will hold in-depth knowledge of the family. No matter how skilled the social worker and no matter how strong the relationship with the client is, we cannot avoid that the families we work with are going to meet the system on the day their social worker isn't in. If you've ever worked in a duty office, you know that you rarely have the time to read the case recordings (assuming they are on file and would tell you something meaningful) before leaving on a duty visit. More often than not, you grab a manager in the hall and get the 'script'.

A parent with clinical depression and features of bi-polar personality disorder struggles to provide basic care to her toddler. She requires long-term support from children's services in the context of an often fragile relationship with her keyworker. When the toddler arrives in nursery one morning sobbing, with a still bleeding cut above his swollen eye, the mother drops him off abruptly and leaves.

An investigation must be undertaken. In the absence of the keyworker, a duty worker begins the process of arranging a strategy discussion, a visit to the child and, subsequently, the parent, a medical and substantial paperwork, likely over a couple of days. This takes place in the context of 'known information', specifically, the mother's mental health diagnosis and poor engagement with the community mental health team. The investigation, not surprisingly, is inconclusive, with no clear picture emerging of what happened. While both parent and child say he 'fell', no understanding is reached about the child's distress and the mother's lack of concern for him. On the keyworker's return, she is faced with an angry parent who refuses to open the door and a child who no longer attends nursery.

In a social work unit, even if the keyworker is on leave, the investigation unfolds differently. A social worker who knows the family well from unit meetings rings the police for a telephone discussion while the children's practitioner, who has a familiar relationship with the toddler, attends the nursery first thing in the morning. The toddler confides that his mother pushed him over on the way to school. The social worker who knows the mother from a visit when the consultant social worker was away attends the mother's home with a police officer. When she introduces herself and the police officer, the mother turns away from the door and walks into the flat. The social worker follows and explains that her consultant social worker is on leave and reminds her of their earlier visit. She shares that she is aware that the mother has been doing a great job getting her son to nursery a few times in the past couple of weeks, and notes that this must have been particularly difficult with her nearby sister away on holiday. The mother responds that her sister isn't due back for another week and she doesn't think she can manage without her. Through these details about the family, even in the absence of the mother's keyworker, the parent experiences something continuous in her relationship with albeit a less familiar part of the system. Within the context of some trust that she is understood, she can explain that she did not feel like getting up today, was late getting her son ready for nursery, and was frustrated by the child's wandering on their way to school. She put her hand on his back to hurry him and he tripped and fell, banging his eye on the pavement. She was upset and annoyed and felt it best to drop him off and leave rather than risk a further outburst towards her son.

The mother agrees to travel to the medical clinic, where the children's practitioner will meet them with her son for a medical, arranged by the unit coordinator. The visits to other families in the unit are rescheduled by the unit coordinator, and key events relating to the investigation are noted in the child's file.

In this example, the investigation is done within a day, and is set in the context of broader work with the family – developing a morning routine that ends with the toddler's arrival at nursery and the mother already in the community where she can run errands and visit family. Important information about the mother's vulnerabilities and need for support is gathered, strengths in her narrative about the morning's events are acknowledged and changes in the support plan can be implemented.

The reality of individual casework in traditional systems is that it can take days, not hours, to complete an investigation, and even if the caseworker is available, they must prioritise medical and police liaison as these can take multiple calls over a couple of hours to arrange. They are unable to respond as quickly to the child whose recall of the event loses accuracy with each re-telling. By the time the interview with the parent is arranged, the importance of the parent's experience in the moment of the incident is lost and is often complicated by their anxiety building over the course of the day or days.

While a skilful practitioner can effectively undertake a duty investigation in a way that minimises the client's experience of being investigated by someone unknown to them, our most helpful tool against this unnecessary imbalance of power is the fluidity and continuity provided by the unit structure.

Attending to multiple processes

Tied closely to this idea of continuity and fluidity is recognition that there are always multiple processes unfolding within a family (and agency) at any time. It is very difficult for one person to attend to all of these processes and experiences effectively. Bearing in mind the many hats that social workers wear and the reality that families within a caseload do not coordinate with each other when they will need support, it is unrealistic to expect that a single individual could effectively attend to all members of the family and all the family processes with equal skill, energy and effectiveness.

Yet, it is crucial that both parents and children are heard, understood and supported. It is important that we have a broad range of skills sets to offer families and that we are available when they need us most. This is one of the unit's greatest assets.

Jo was the eldest daughter in a large sibling group. Our work with the family was informed by a mother's detailed account of the family history which included sexual violence towards adults and children over multiple generations. She was keen to work alongside the unit to protect herself and her children from further violence. There was much to be done within a short period of time, to address the most acute needs. The home needed immediate improvements, the children had immediate medical needs to attend to, there were risk assessments to be done on known offenders within the family network, household routines to establish, major financial difficulties, substance misuse intervention to be arranged, alternate carers to be assessed. Our children's practitioner was tasked with getting to know the children, their interests, strengths, anxieties, supportive relationships and so on. There were family support workers, health professionals, housing officers; the list of people involved with the family went on. While we had good people on hand, I was concerned about the number of professionals involved with the family, and how the children in particular would make sense of this.

Jo was 12. She dressed like a boy, sauntered like a boy and did her best to make herself invisible. On our first meeting, I unwittingly called her by her older brother's name. While she presented as shy, she was bright and, if you can be at 12, savvy. In the absence of both our social worker and children's practitioner one day, I had to attend Jo's school after she had suffered a serious injury to her leg the night before. We had met only once before, but she recognised me and we chatted briefly about her children's practitioner being away today and then how her football club was going. I looked at her leg and she told me about the trip to A&E and reiterated her 'falling down the stairs' story verbatim as it was recorded in the medical notes. As I was preparing to leave and feeling a little disheartened, trying to imagine how we would possibly go about developing some kind of trust with this young girl amidst all the other work happening in the family, she lifted her chin and almost whispered to me from behind the long fringe poking out under her cap: 'Karen,' she said, 'is Simonne for me?' I smiled, nodded and told her confidently and with great relief, 'Yes, she is just for you and she'll see you on Friday.'

Summary

Social work has always been about relationships, and Reclaiming Social Work is about bringing relationships back to the forefront of our work. In doing so, it is important to remember that relationships require more than just our best intentions; they require availability and continuity, they require distractions kept to a minimum and they require that we don't slip into bad habits when under pressure. It is more than just finding the right people to do a difficult job and equipping them with skills; it is about a whole systems change that enables us to do our best work.

I hope that I have outlined here that while we want to be therapeutic and spend time co-constructing reality with families in the hope of enabling change, in the context of statutory child protection work there are things, big things, which are going to get in the way. These examples begin to demonstrate that the unit model within Reclaiming Social Work has created a unique and highly effective system for:

- creating an accessible, continuous and reliable sub-space for families within a large bureaucracy which can mobilise resources and navigate other systems

- maintaining the momentum and integrity of statutory and therapeutic processes in the face of staff absences and turnover

- attending to multiple processes within the same family

- ensuring that small voices, voices that have been silent for a long time, get heard.

Commentary by Professor Stephen Scott

This chapter explores an often hidden aspect of effective therapeutic work: what structures are necessary to support the social worker to form an effective relationship with a client. We have already heard about useful theoretical formulations for understanding families, including social learning theory (SLT) and a systemic approach, and this chapter adds two important elements: first of all, the importance of basic interpersonal human understanding, and second, the importance of having structures around one that enable one to develop this effectively. The author points out that if you are to engage with a family and have their trust, which is going to be essential to lead on to more effective interventions, then you have to be able to understand them.

The chapter describes how a close-knit unit of five people who exchange information about cases can lead to a much more continuous and understanding level of support for a parent. When the clients ring up, instead of getting a duty person who knows nothing about them, they get somebody who is familiar with the broad outline of their case and can help sort things out effectively and quickly. This sounds ideal, but before advocating this approach it would be useful to know at what cost this comes, as it must take time to update colleagues with each of your cases, and in a very pressured and busy environment, it must take some nerve to do this. I firmly believe that this is a desirable process, but acknowledging the need for teams to create the space to do this would perhaps make it more exportable to other teams who would like to take the Reclaiming Social Work approach. The author makes the point that once individuals feel trusted, they are far more likely to reveal the truth of the situation, which in turn can lead to more sensitive and effective interventions. What shines through the personal examples are first, having quick responses, second, the strengths-based approach whereby families' intentions and efforts to do the right thing and their capabilities are fully acknowledged and developed, and third, the emphasis on understanding the client's narrative.

The author is clear that the real work is 'relationship building, co-constructing problems and enabling change'. This last bit is absolutely crucial, and sometimes it seems that less effective social work is only focusing on the first two, making a 'nice' relationship with families, avoiding the need to do statutory work and to set firm limits and represent outside society in an 'authoritarian' way, often then not leading to effective change. Sometimes it feels that some workers want to be a family's friend, and cannot take on the fact that their clients may be the children who may need to be protected, and like in any realistic relationship, this will involve some limit setting and not just being 'nice'. It is always important when applying such models to be clear about what one wishes to change and to focus on it relentlessly, otherwise one can drift into a fog of general and unclear practice.

This chapter shows how by having a supportive and coherent team around the practitioner they are then liberated to do satisfying and effective work. I suspect this approach is central to building staff morale and satisfaction, and results in a low turnover of staff. These are measurable constructs, and were noted to be present in the independent review of the Hackney approach (Cross *et al.* 2010). We now need solid research to confirm this; the findings will further promote the wider dissemination of the Reclaiming Social Work model.

References
Cross, S., Hubbard, A. and Munro, E. (2010) *Reclaiming Social Work: London Borough of Hackney's Children and Young People's Services, Parts 1 and 2.* London: Human Reliability Associates and London School of Economics and Political Science.

CHAPTER 7

Working with People in Transition[1]

Timo Dobrowolski

A Wednesday afternoon in East London's autumn. It is cold outside but cosy and warm here in this flat. The conversation is going well. Child practitioner Kerrie and I are beginning to feel that we are getting somewhere with Ruby and Deirdre. Ruby agrees that she is not exactly behaving in any angelic way, and we start working on solutions. Finally, we find a unified strategy, and then…

Deirdre yells, 'Get the fuck out of my house!!!'

Ruby replies by slamming the door. Both of us are simply stunned and silenced by this outburst. End of story…for this Wednesday.

My name is Timo Dobrowolski. I am a consultant social worker in Hackney and I once graduated in social pedagogy/social work in Germany. Usually, when I introduce myself to families, I call myself a social worker, although my influences from social pedagogy play a huge part in my daily work.

Generally speaking, I understand social pedagogy as a perspective that is less interested in symptoms than in causes. It is more community based and preventative than the classical social work model as it is commonly practised in the UK. Social pedagogy ties in perfectly with systemic theory and practice as the systemic school too is by far more interested in the causation of problems within social networks than in answering them with quick-fix interventions such as criminalising and imprisoning or accommodating children – solutions that are found at the very end of downward spirals. In Reclaiming Social Work, in systemic practice and in social pedagogy we are interested in all the steps and analyses that come before those heavy-handed measures.

---

1   Names, apart from those of professionals, have been changed to protect anonymity.

Our unit is part of what is called 'Rapid Response'. We are 'rapid' as we try – depending on the availability of our clients – to respond to referrals immediately, that is, on the day the referral is being received. When parents or their children ask me what we do, I tend to say that we are a service that either works with young people that are 'on the brink of going into care' or youngsters that are living with a friend, relative, etc. I would then go on to explain that our main tasks are to reunite and/or stabilise families in acute crises – this crisis aspect is the reason why immediate intervention is what we have been offering as those first hours can prevent lengthy periods of children residing in foster care arrangements. Usually, when I explain our unit's goals and strategies, I add that we work with whole families as opposed to working with individuals. As Reclaiming Social Work is based on working in a systemic fashion, this focus plays a significant role, and I will demonstrate that this is more than a big word in our unit's daily practice. With the following vignette I try to show that working in a systemic way is an arduous, intense and holistic approach that includes working with a young person's micro-system, the core family and the macro-systems, which might be the young person's friends, their school, the local police force and any other significant influence. On average, our interventions take three to six months.

We work with teenagers. So why did I not choose the topic 'Working with teenagers'? To answer this question we need to take a look at the inherent processes of transitional stages, that is, the realignment processes of whole social systems that go hand in hand with one individual's process of change – namely here, this is the teenage daughter's battle for increasing independence and less parental control and her social environment's reactions.

Most explanations we use for this transitional period called 'youth' will describe:

- Rites of passage, which are different in different cultures. In the Western world this might entail belonging to a youth culture and sporting urban-tribalistic symbolisms that demonstrate belonging. Also, this includes school exams as a rite of entry into the world of paid labour.

- Physical changes – that is, 'puberty' as a causation for gender identity and role behaviours.

- A distancing from the parents' care.

During this process many parents experience a high level of frustration for numerous reasons. There might be a narcissistic component of feeling less needed when caring was a parent's very role definition. Moreover, there might be clashes of values and opinions, the so-called 'generation gap' between the growing child's new attitudes and the parent's unchanged points of view. Many teenagers suffer under the contradictions between their parents' and their peers' behavioural demands. Nowadays, many teenagers possibly feel frustrated because they miss this generation gap when parents themselves become older teenagers, but to discuss this problem another chapter would be required.

As you can see, this is a complex transition and social work in this field focuses on the re-negotiation of parental expectations and teenagers' behaviour.

Ruby, as you might have guessed, is one of the two key players in the middle of this transitional process. When we initially met her she was 14 years old. She is quite an outspoken girl of mixed Caribbean and White Irish heritage. Her equally outspoken mother, Deirdre, our second key player, is White Irish, and her father, Delroy, is of Caribbean descent. Delroy, however, has not been on the scene for most of Ruby's life. Deirdre survives on benefits. During the time of our involvement Ruby was sharing a two-bedroom flat with her in a deprived city area. Ruby, as many teenagers in East London and elsewhere, was on the periphery of a gang that controls huge parts of the local drug trade. During our work with this family we found out that there was a multi-generational pattern of children going into care on the maternal side of the family – a cycle that we decidedly endeavoured to break. This pattern was part of Deirdre's own childhood history.

Most significantly our unit's child practitioner, Kerrie, and I noticed the emotional temperature in this mother–daughter dyad. There was door slamming and swearing from both sides and after Ruby stormed off halfway through the first interview we heard words like 'she would open her legs for everybody' coming from her mother's mouth. The case notes read:

> …I got the impression that Ruby is currently trying to test whether she really is being cared for by her mother; after she had left the house she came back in again and shouted that her mother should not report her missing. However, to me this sounded as if she was demanding that her mother did exactly this because there would have been no other reason to re-enter the flat. I later discussed

with Kerrie that we both felt an impulse to run after her, which is in line with my hypothesis that Ruby is provoking concerns to test whether people are caring about her.

I have always found working hypotheses useful. They might be wrong, they can be discussed and corrected or even dismissed at all times, but they are a starting point from which the journey into a deeper understanding of families can commence. Without a starting hypothesis social work easily becomes a tiresome exercise in reacting to symptomatic behaviour. Hence, a starting hypothesis should always be a draft of an understanding of why a family acts in their own specific ways. With this preliminary explanation in mind, social work can become an effective tool with a long-term goal based on hypothesis. Those hypotheses are formulated together with the family so that feedback about change is possible in a mutual understanding, rather than in one where an outside expert has diagnosed a family to prescribe a cure. The hypothesis 'She is running away to make you feel worried because she wants to feel loved' was shared with Deirdre, and this created a creative conflict with her hypothesis 'She is doing this to provoke me.' In this kind of creative conflict new meanings and new ways forward are created *in a joint venture*.

What were Ruby's hypotheses about the situation? To find out we decided – under the guidance and advice of our family therapist, Amanda – that Kerrie would take Ruby for a burger. Ruby had expressed that she found meetings boring so we thought this might bring a bit of excitement into her view of social work practice. Well, unfortunately Ruby was not a fan of child practitioners and social workers alike, and we soon realised that having lunch was more our wish than hers.

During one home visit Kerrie and I were drawn into detailed descriptions about contraceptive methods and Ruby's sexual relationships with older teenage males. In the background, there was a protesting Ruby who tearfully demanded that her mother stop sharing all this information with strangers. She became even more tearful when I had a short one-to-one with her in the kitchen where she told me that her mother had told everybody in the family that she has a contraceptive implant. Hence, a further hypothesis was that the family had very thin boundaries and that Ruby was suffering immensely under this situation. It also became increasingly clear that Deirdre appeared to have severe difficulties controlling her angry outbursts.

Another significant event was when Deirdre decided to call me to announce that she was going to kill herself by jumping off a local bridge, which is in line with and most likely an expression of her difficulties to deal with her emotions in a calm(er) manner. Also, I would like to hypothesise that this was an expression of not having had good-enough parental role models that would have provided Deirdre with a inner template of coping strategies that would not manifest themselves in these louder performative acts such as arguments, suicide threats or the announced intention to put her own daughter into care. What had happened to cause this threat? I do not want to under-estimate Deirdre's stress levels by saying that nothing much had happened apart from the fact that Ruby had stayed out late again. However, Deirdre's reaction to this struck the unit as erratic and disproportionate. But who am I to say what normal human behaviour is? Anyway, not long after Deirdre's phone call, which put me back into the role of a social controller – one undeniable aspect of social work – I felt obliged to dial 999. Arriving on the scene, the familiar sense of chaos and emotional upheaval was awaiting Kerrie and me. There were two police officers, ambulance staff, a tearful Ruby and a shouting Deirdre. The ambulance staff soon left, but it took some debating skills and persistence to convince the police officers to leave. At this point in time we felt trapped because Deirdre had spoken those magic words: 'I am going to hit her!' As we had had several encounters with her we felt confident that we could have a discussion that would lead us all into a calmer situation. This opinion was based on the fact that we had shared several points of view with Deirdre and we now thought we had an understanding of what was going on. It was usually this point, when Deirdre felt understood, that she became more approachable. Kerrie mainly focused on this calming conversation while I was trying to reason with Ruby, who kindly gave me permission to enter her bedroom. The picture that is conjured up in my mind is that of diplomats negotiating between warring parties. Ruby would not stop calling friends on her mobile phone, planning her next trip into the wilderness while I was talking to her. We finally managed to persuade Ruby to stay with her aunt Rhian and, in all honesty, this had no other purpose than giving mother and daughter a 'breather'.

Ruby was quite talkative and even in a kind of happy mood when we took her to her aunt. We all sat down and I started to explain why Ruby needed Rhian's support. Rhian was agreeable to letting Ruby stay for a while. We fortunately also met Rhian's partner, Rico. He explained openly that he had been a heroin user and that he had been living on the street. This we used as an intervention in itself, and asked Rico whether he could tell Ruby about his experiences. He agreed and we left.

Rhian had been a drug user too, and still had social work support. When we phoned her social worker as part of our routine checks she expressed concerns but did not think that it was impossible for Ruby to stay with Rhian for a while. Children who grow up in care have disadvantages not only in terms of the label they carry but also because of the statistically proven negative outcomes in terms of their overall life situation. To rather place a child with a family member who is an ex-drug user than in foster care is the direct consequence of those findings.

However, the whole arrangement collapsed after approximately one week. Rhian phoned us and declared that she had had enough of Ruby's attitude and her staying out late. Despite Ruby's resolutions she was simply continuing her own special programme.

There were many times when we did not know where Ruby was at all. Sometimes she stayed with a friend we knew; sometimes she was back home. Her lifestyle was beginning to become a precise mirroring of the chaotic relationship with her mum. When Ruby's whereabouts were unknown, we cooperated with the local police's Missing Persons Unit and phoned Ruby every other day. Despite Ruby's negative attitude towards the unit I am sure that this gave her stability.

Against our overall goal to break the above-mentioned trans-generational cycle, my senior manager and I came to the agreement that we would be offering Ruby a foster placement as we thought that the situation was getting out of control. Having received information from Ruby's school that she was 'shotting' drugs (acting as a drug courier) and that she allegedly had had sex with older teenage males, we became anxious. Strangely enough, it was Ruby herself – she had initially expressed the wish to go into care – who sabotaged all three attempts to accommodate her. Either she would not turn up at our office, saying that the chosen placement was too far away (although it was in the neighbouring borough), or she would use other, admittedly quite clever, techniques.

One day she said she would meet me in a public place at 7 p.m. but did not turn up. When I phoned her she said she was in a local park, which is known as a hang-out for a certain gang with a certain reputation. Weighing up my safety and her apparent level of motivation to be accompanied to her new foster placement, I quickly made the decision to go home. Another time she tricked us by coming to our office, saying she would go to a reintegration meeting at her school, leaving a bag with personal belongings as a surety that she was coming back while our fostering department was still searching for a placement. She even managed to use the school by officially arranging an appointment. She never came back, and needless to say our fostering department's social workers became increasingly annoyed. However, there was one positive during this day. Before Ruby left our office I had breakfast with her in a local cafe. Despite the stroppy attitude she gave towards the staff, there was yet a completely new side I observed in her character. She instantly spotted a singing plastic fish that was pinned to the wall, told me proudly that she knew what this fish could do and asked me whether she could show me. To do this she even surprisingly kindly asked the staff whether she could press 'the button'. When this peculiar piece of decoration finally began to sing Ruby was smiling all over her face and I was chuckling away. This moment revealed all of Ruby's childishness that was usually masked by her hard street kid attitude, and despite the fact that Ruby's life did not become more stabilised that day, I was glad that I was sharing this little moment with her.

As the situation continued to be chaotic we decided that an increase of the unit's influence on a community level was required. Systemic practice allows us to invite as many people as useful and required into the process of change because only a change in the wider system would secure long-lasting improvements. The argument here is that individuals and smaller family systems, like this mother–daughter dyad, can create new solutions. However, if this change gets lost in the wider context, the risk of returning to old maladaptive behaviours is high.

The revised strategy took different forms.

During a school meeting we made it clear that we would not accommodate Ruby any more. This unleashed a storm of protest among the other professionals. However, Kerrie, our newly arrived social worker, Tonia, and I were sure that accommodating Ruby would not work anyway. We convinced the school staff of our point of view by showing the wider picture of the difficulties that Ruby had – that her absconding was not an isolated event but one in a history of other problematic behaviours that had their roots in her relationship with her mother and that an effective intervention could only be based on a change within this relationship.

Meetings between the school and Ruby became a regular event.

Furthermore, we intensified our contact with one of Ruby's friends' mothers. This family appeared to be committed to Ruby's well-being and had provided her with a bed on numerous occasions. When Ruby's school friend's behaviour – which had been very much like Ruby's – improved, we had a golden systemic opportunity. This school friend's mother had told us that her daughter had recently told Ruby to return home. We positively reinforced this by telling this mother that she should tell her daughter that the whole unit was very grateful for her efforts.

On the other end of the spectrum I started to assert pressure. One evening when I phoned Ruby's mobile phone another friend answered it. I told this friend straight away that 'harbouring a minor' was a crime and that the police was certainly interested why Ruby had left her mobile phone in her possession. This aspect of our now strengthened strategy I would call *making running away as uncomfortable as possible*, and if I would have to find a theoretical framework for this, I would call it 'social cognitive behavioural therapy' (CBT).

Our family therapist, Amanda, and I continued to have therapeutic sessions with Deirdre. Those revealed not only Deirdre's helplessness and disappointment, which resulted from numerous broken relationships, but Deirdre's own sister presented as a huge obstacle during this process as she would not stop encouraging Deirdre to kick Ruby out. The language she used while doing this was derogatory and abusive. I took the decision to give direct feedback about the language and to exclude this aunt from the process, and to ask her not to be present when I was talking to Deirdre. Systemic work not only means understanding and engaging the whole system; it also means identifying the counter-productive factors in the system and making clear decisions as to how to deal with negative influences. A sentence that we now began to repeat like a Tibetan mantra was 'We are not going to accommodate your daughter. You have parental responsibility.' Believe me, this was not well received.

There was another intermediate period where Ruby's other aunt, Jacqui, became her temporary carer. This aunt I had motivated to contact Ruby in two extensive chats. Those chats also shed more light on the family history. There were previous requests by Deirdre to accommodate her two older daughters when they were teenagers. However happy we were about this intermediate arrangement, Ruby stole clothes and money from Jacqui after just four days.

It appeared like a little wonder but at this point, when we all thought things could not get any worse, I phoned Deirdre who simply said, 'She is here.' This sentence invoked a six-month period of calm in which Ruby started to attend alternative schooling and mostly stayed at home. We did become involved again, but in this chapter I only want to focus on those first five months.

To me it stands out as an important fact that the unit's general mood at this point in time could be described as exhaustion and annoyance. It took all five unit members one or two weeks to realise that we had finally succeeded.

What did we learn during this time?

Well, the first fact is simple but nevertheless important. *It takes patience to do systemic social work.* This kind of patience involves not being liked by other professionals while going against the grain and explaining things over and over again, sticking to one's decisions while being flexible enough to change the course of action if safety issues arise. This patience also includes not being liked by the family members with whom you are working. This dislike, in my view, arises from the fact that social workers are trying to break well-rehearsed behaviours that are maladaptive but nevertheless give families a sense of security. We all have fears of the unknown, and when we break away from family dynamics we are doing exactly this: we invoke fear and this inadvertently provokes resistance.

The second fact is similarly simple and similarly important: *systemic social work is exhausting.* It requires a sensitive and humorous unit or team to make up for the stress of the individual worker. Working with an outside system is strongly influenced by the internal relationships in a unit. It is crucial that the whole unit continuously discusses and reviews the course of action and that the individual worker has the same goal as the rest of the unit. Otherwise, going against the grain becomes an impossible exercise that would potentially burn colleagues out. However, Hackney operates a policy of 'transfer windows' should a practitioner feel stuck and temporarily overburdened. In practice this means that an internal application for a post in another field can prevent burn-out and, therefore, enhance staff retainment. While a transfer to another field of work is rather a last measure of supporting staff, I would also like to mention that the Reclaiming Social Work model frees up far more time for emotional staff support than allowed for in the traditional model. Time that is usually spent on reflection on cases is being shifted to the weekly unit meetings, while supervision sessions can focus far more on individual staff development. In our model of work, supervision is a core factor for successful retainment of emotional resources.

I would like to add that systemic social work requires the individual practitioner's conviction to break with certain social work practices, for example, the tendency to accommodate children when long-term work could prevent this by making changes within families possible.

The third fact is: *systemic social work brings about change.* However, for this change to become possible there needs to be enough stubbornness from the unit/team to enable the family to rehearse actions in newly created realities. There is no point in giving clever advice and quickly pulling out. We need to dance with the families for a while until they have learned their new steps.

The fourth fact is a bit more complicated. In hindsight, I am wondering what the factor was that caused the changes in Ruby to coincide with the change of the whole family system. Maybe I could call this fact *internal changes cause systemic changes.* My first question in this context is, what does it mean for a mother who has had many unsatisfactory and/or painful relationships, which must have impacted on her self-esteem, that her daughter starts to show (verbally and through actions) that she wants more distance and independence? The second more general question is whether all parents feel rejected and hurt when they understand that they are less needed, and how much influence the parent's self-esteem has on the capacity to cope with those hurtful emotions. The relationship between one's self-esteem and the capacity to cope with those feelings appears to be based on the creation of social meaning(s). What kind of meaning have significant relationships had for Deirdre? Or for the rest of the family? How much does a child become the rescuer of the mother's self-esteem should the previous relationships have failed, and lead to feelings of worthlessness and failure? How does the task of being a mother ensure that the thought 'I am not wanted' does not re-emerge?

On a more general basis, the families we are working with usually make one important shift: from a position of strongly imagined impossibilities to remain united as a child(ren)-parent unit to the experience of having worked through their crises *together.* This in itself provides a memorable experience and a memorable resource for future crises in each family member's mind. In this context I would like to point to the theory of radical constructivism (Watzlawick 1984), which is one major influence in the current systemic landscape. The meaning 'I cannot live with my child (or parent, from the child's perspective)' is constructed by a context of messages and meanings stemming from (wider) family dynamics and the families' histories, the very fact that we live in a culture that offers foster and residential care (with all its appropriateness when children are at risk of significant harm), the media and the way teenagers are currently portrayed, the narratives teenagers come up with themselves in their peer groups, etc.

Deconstructing meanings, that is, deconstructing those aspects with family members in order to create new narratives, for example from problem-saturated to resources-oriented ones, is a core element of our work.

It appears that a social work unit that works stubbornly through those crises with a family almost becomes like a crutch, without which the family could not walk through times in which old pains are reactivated through change.

A last word about Ruby and Deirdre. They did come back. After about six months the family was re-referred in a state of emotional turmoil that reminded me strongly of our previous times with them. However, this time it only took three weeks of intense intervention until things were calmer again. And here is my fifth fact.

Systemic social work creates sustainability. Expressed in figures this meant that between April 2010 and April 2011 less than 9 per cent of the cases worked on by Rapid Response required referrals/transfers to other services, which in turn meant that our final assessment in those cases outside these 9 per cent was that the families had developed enough independent strategies to go through potential future challenges. Part of Reclaiming Social Work is an ongoing statistical measuring of our impact on families. This nicely leads to the last fact.

Systemic social work is cost-effective because it makes change possible in a wider context than individual client-focused work. Not only does systemic working allow the breaking up of multi-generational patterns, but it also enables change on wider family levels. Hence the number of behavioural relapses and (re-)referrals decreases.

Let us take another quick look at numbers.

Of 73 families worked on in Rapid Response during 2009, 69 were successfully prevented from coming into long-term care, a success rate of 94.5 per cent (Hackney Children and Young People's Services 2010).

Of 86 cases worked on in Rapid Response during 2010, 77 children were successfully prevented from becoming looked after, a success rate of 91 per cent.

Seen from the angle of annual costs for local authorities, these numbers are proof for an effective decrease in public spending we managed to achieve long before the current government's spending policies came into effect (the interested reader might want to take a look at the report

The Costs of Foster Care, jointly published by The Fostering Network and the British Association of Adoption and Fostering (BAAF) in 2010.

A wider view

After one-and-a-half years, I am now able to see recurring tendencies in this field of social work.

One of those tendencies is that we have mostly been working with teenage girls. The change of traditional gender modes appears to have caused changes in stereotypical gender-related behaviours. A gang, for example, does not appear to be a place for sole male bonding and competition. On the contrary, we do have pure girls' gangs in East London. The decline of the traditional mother-father-child family appears to have made it increasingly difficult for teenagers to be in receipt of enough affection, stability and care, especially when their single carers work. Gangs act like surrogate families. Knowing this, it would be inexcusable to dismiss gangs simply as a bad influence and nuisance in the community. They are strong social systems with all the potential advantages and disadvantages of such a system.

A further tendency I have observed is that most of the family conflicts coincide with a lack of resources in the wider family. This does not always mean that there are no available family members. The crucial factor is not the availability of family members but their lacking (= not yet developed) competence. In families that have been dysfunctional for generations, maladaptive coping mechanisms appear to be multiplied across the whole system. Often it takes a long time to find family members who are the exception from this rule.

Commentary by Professor Stephen Scott

This chapter gives in some detail the example of applying a systemic approach to a teenage girl who was on the edge of coming into care. The girl in question, Ruby, is out of the control of her mother, who herself is part of an intergenerational pattern of children going into care. Ruby is at risk in many ways, often going missing, sometimes mixing with drug gangs, and sometimes going off to live with her aunt, as well as putting herself at risk sexually with older men.

The author shows how having the hypothesis (in this case that Ruby was testing limits to see if her mother loved her enough to come after her) is an essential guide to action. It also shows how by hanging in for several months, the social worker was eventually, to some extent, able to take the role of parent, for example dialling 999 to get the police, arranging meetings with the school, and so on, to start finally putting some containment around this vulnerable 14-year-old. Perhaps what is most striking about this case is the courage and nerve of the social worker not to accommodate the child who seemed to be very at risk, but instead he firmly places the problem back with the parent, and says that her mother has responsibility.

Although the mechanism of change isn't described, the reader is led to believe that through this approach the mother did take some responsibility for her daughter as she did succeed in living at home with her and had a six-month period of relative calm, during which time she attended school and mostly stayed at home. The author takes the mature stance of being able to accept that he might not be liked by the client he is working with, and has the tenacity to hang in there for several months, plugging away at useful interventions, in the faith that change will come. This is an important lesson, as many difficult families that one sees with complex needs are often a case of two steps forward and one, or sometimes two or three, steps back. By persisting and putting the right structures and relationships in place, however, gradual improvement is often seen.

Here the author shows how when he worked the different elements of the system (other relatives, schools and the police when necessary), the girl in question could be contained sufficiently to feel loved and thrive adequately back at home. It seems likely that if the effort had simply been to try to improve the relationship between mother and daughter, the girl would have been at much higher risk as she was out for a lot of the time at that stage, or if she had been taken into care, the mother never would have found the confidence to parent rather more effectively and skilfully. This would have been less cost-effective too, as taking children into care is very expensive – low needs children cost on average £33,000 per year in care, high needs £101,000 per year (Ward, Holmes and Soper 2008). Then there may be further costs – in the London borough I work in, there are 18 16- and 17-year-old girls placed in children's homes. Each year half of them get pregnant, and taking their babies into care costs £100,000 each.

What seems to be one of the factors that enabled the author to carry on is his acknowledgement that such work is indeed exhausting and sometimes painful – at times you feel frustrated and angry and unappreciated by a family. However, the author is very clear that the social worker is not there to feed his need to be liked, and therefore ploughs on in a professional manner, with the support of his team. Sadly many teams do not acknowledge the difficulty of the work or the emotional reactions that such heart-wrenching families can have on the individual, which then leads rapidly to burn-out, and more automated forms of social work practice, whereby forms are filled and boxes ticked, but the essential relationships leading to change are not maintained.

How could one further build on this model? First, by specifying the nature of supervision, and what goes on during supervision; second, by specifying how hypotheses change as one gets more information about a family; and third, how one sets specific targets. Thus in this case the targets might have been to get the mother to provide better supervision of her daughter by finding out where she was and rewarding her when she came home and giving her sanctions when she did not; to get mother and daughter to have a positive time together, say, once a week; to negotiate between the aunt and the mother who would be looking after her and when; and so on. By taking a measurable approach to outcomes, the work can become more focused and this can be liberating to workers, rather than just trying to stand up in a hail of complexities and disasters and criticism from families and other professionals when things go wrong.

Like the other chapters, this contribution shows how good social work requires both a strong intellect and a strong heart. Strong intellect is needed to understand what is going on, which is different in every family and needs not only good assessment but also good judgement as to what are the core elements, and good heart to carry on and carry out good interventions, even when the situation seems disheartening and others are critical.

References

Hackney Children and Young People's Services (2010) *Annual Report 2009, Looked After Children*. London: Hackney Children and Young People's Services.

The Fostering Network and the British Association of Adoption and Fostering (BAAF) (2010) *The Costs of Foster Care: Investing in Our Children's Future*. Available at www.fostering.net/sites/www.fostering.net/files/public/resources/reports/cofc_report. pdf, accessed on 1 July 2011.

Ward, H., Holmes, L. and Soper, J. (2008) *Costs and Consequences of Placing Children in Care*. London: Jessica Kingsley Publishers.

Watzlawick, P. (ed.) (1984) *The Invented Reality. How Do We Know What We Believe We Know?* New York: Norton.

CHAPTER 8

The Centrality of Relationships

Karen Gaughan and Sonya Kalyniak

Introduction

We are two social work professionals who began our positions as consultant social workers in Hackney Leaving Care Service approximately two years ago. This was a new role for both of us and a different experience in many ways from our previous social work positions. It was the first time in line management and a first new experience in the newly developed role of consultant social worker. Immediately after starting, we both enrolled in a postgraduate systemic therapy course. Throughout our experience we have reflected frequently about how to apply the theory and technique learned to our social work units and the work we do with our care leavers and their families. This way of working has evolved over the past two years, and this chapter is an opportunity to reflect on how the position has changed us as practitioners and challenged us to take our practice to a different level. The clearest shift throughout this journey has been looking closely at the importance of relationships in the work we do, and how systemic ideas have pushed us to think about relationships in a different way. This is true not only with our young people, but with members of the unit and the wider professional system.

How relationships are formed differently

When thinking about what is enabling us to develop richer and more helpful relationships with young people we need to highlight what we are doing differently as units to enable this to occur. In traditional casework teams, individual workers are allocated their cases and solely responsible for thinking about how to work with them. Of course, workers have opportunities to talk with managers within supervision; however, this can invariably result in listing the tasks that have been done with limited time for reflection or suggestions of how to move forward with a particular young person or difficult issues. Despite receiving well intentioned support from colleagues, when dealing with challenging cases, many workers continue to relate to the overwhelming feeling of being 'stuck' with a young person. This sometimes means being unsure of how to manage presenting behaviours or feeling unable to make progress with them. Within the Reclaiming Social Work model there has been an experience of a more shared sense of commitment in relation to not leaving one person individually to think, reflect and come up with planned responses. Instead, there is a real commitment to bringing forth multi-perspectives from all unit members when thinking about cases, and for unit members to support each other through collaborative weekly discussion, joint visits and several unit members working directly with the young person if felt appropriate. This way of working opens up opportunities to be creative, to see situations from various angles, and it goes some way to breaking negative patterns of interaction and 'un-sticking' cases. By looking at a young person through a variety of lenses and trying to get a sense of the whole person through case discussion and systemic techniques, it encourages workers to move from a static impression of the young person.

In individual casework, cases can arise that are incredibly stressful and draining for one person to work with individually, but unit working allows these cases to feel less daunting. For example, one case involved working with a mixed heritage 18-year-old male struggling to budget due to spending money on drugs and struggling to maintain his accommodation due to challenging behaviour. Individually, a caseworker would be bombarded with visits and phone calls requesting money. However, due to the unit style of working and many members having developed a relationship with the young person, we were able to share the responsibility for dealing with this young person and support each other under stressful circumstances. This supportive type of environment helps avoid staff burn-out and also reduces the likelihood of the worker being enmeshed with the family system and becoming part of the problem rather than the solution (Burnham 1986).

Working as a unit allows for different types of relationships to develop, both with young people and colleagues. Dallos and Draper (2005) argue that teamwork provides creative and supportive experiences which embody a second order cybernetic stance. Jones (1993) highlights the far reaching capabilities of the 'group mind', creating new narratives where 'infinitely new possibilities can be constructed in a way that is often more far ranging, and discontinuous, than the solutions or insights striven for by the therapists working in other modalities or (alone)' (p.50). The unit provides an opportunity for these ideas to come to life within a social work setting. The unit style of working invites us to nurture individual talents, experiences, knowledge, and to value individuals who attempt to depart from set ideas. This results in contributing to new ideas and often new meanings can emerge in group discussion.

The unit allows for conversations that can mean moving from a set image of a young person to thinking more creatively about what is happening in their life. One 18-year-old young person was displaying challenging and demanding behaviour and seeming to refuse to take any responsibility for himself. He was not able to maintain benefit claims, pay rent or manage his money. As a unit, we hypothesised that it may be his perception of himself as still a 'child', that he still needed to be looked after by appropriate adults in his life. His ideas about what parents, or those acting as parents, are required to do for him and our ideas about what us as 'corporate parents' are required to do were very different. Moving the unit's perceptions of this young person's behaviour away from descriptions of being demanding and unwilling to take any responsibility meant thinking of this young person in a context which enabled us to see him as wanting desperately to be parented due to having no other familial figures in his life and no one who cared for him. Shifting our discussion with him from the grapple of practical tasks and possible consequences to one connected to the meaning of 'parenting' helped him to see that the unit wanted to continue to offer caring parental support for him. For the unit, this meant supporting him to develop his own resources and skills to manage the practical aspects in life.

Relationships within the unit: a secure base

The unit requires colleagues' willingness to expose individual practice and reflections within a group in order to work more collaboratively (Burnham 1986). Everyone will have an individual response to clients who can be challenging or display socially unacceptable behaviour. Some members of the staff team may empathise more than others depending on what the presenting issues are. At one point, a worker came back from a home visit with a young person and was able to be reflective and transparent enough to express how difficult they would find working with someone presenting racist and misogynist behaviour. This practitioner essentially found it hard to 'like' the young person. The unit meeting enabled more understanding and sympathetic voices to be heard about this young person within the context of their individual lives which enabled a discussion to be had about why this young person may have these views and what the meaning was for him and others. This in turn enabled further discussion about why this young person made such an impact on the worker, utilising Bateson's GRRAACCEESS idea (Batesonn 1978). Through the GRRAACCEESS concept, practitioners are enabled to understand meanings for clients through becoming aware of the influences that may affect the client's unique position within the world. These influences include gender, race, religion, age, ability, class, culture, ethnicity, education, sexuality and spirituality. It is equally important to be mindful of how these influences affect us as workers in relation to our views and responses with clients. This type of discussion seemed rare within a traditional supervision or team meeting before, and it was most enriching. The value of creating a multiverse of possible descriptions and meanings to any given situation opens up possibilities for more positive relationships to form and meaningful support to be given that may not have been previously identified (Young et al. 1997).

These types of occurrences have led to hypothesising about what makes workers feel part of the unit and safe to expose their thoughts, prejudices and weak points of practice. Trust, support and a non-blaming atmosphere are important within the unit dynamics. Indeed, ideas about attachment have helped hypothesis about what is needed to create a secure base of mutual trust, respect and support in order for unit working to thrive. The role of the consultant social worker can perhaps be compared to that of a leader who nurtures an environment so staff feel comfortable in being curious and willing to explore varied hypotheses in respect of young people and their systems. The more secure workers feel within the unit, the less tightly scripted their assessments and responses, which in turn opens up other meanings and ways of moving forward with young people. Utilising systemic ideas about how we are organised in the unit invites a more recursive process inviting feedback.

With hindsight it is possible to see how easy it was to react defensively about personal practice when working in a traditional team. However, social constructionist ideas have enabled an understanding that there is no 'absolute truth' or correct way of doing things; instead, there are only ways that fit at a particular time within a particular context. This has been found to be a valuable way of thinking about practice as it invites us to be learning and reflecting constantly. Of course there remain statutory responsibilities and timescales; however, this work can be done ascetically and creatively. Essentially, it serves to keep us interested and excited about the possibilities of working with young people.

How we behave with and how we talk about young people differently

One of the biggest challenges when starting in a consultant social worker role was trying to understand the lives of the young people with whom the unit would be working. The case histories appeared problem-saturated, and, as in other experiences, the chronologies focused mainly on the significant events, for example placement changes, and what difficulties the young people had experienced in care. Of course, documentation of the young person's challenges in the care system are highly important, but so are the small and large successes that show a young person is moving forward. Some of the histories came across as intimidating, hopeless, scary, impossible and unbelievably challenging. The questions remained as to how, at this stage in the young person's life, could one elicit change? Was there hope for some of the young people who could be seen as an impossible challenge?

It is interesting to read a case file with a sense of unlimited curiosity, a systemic idea that breeds understanding and optimism rather than despair and hopelessness. It helps immensely with keeping an open mind and hearing the young person's story from their perspective. For example, one of the first young people with whom the unit worked was a 19-year-old male just released from prison, with over 30 arrests and seven convictions throughout his adolescence. Naturally there were some hesitations of how to best support this young person, including thinking about personal safety. However, working with this case with a sense of curiosity meant that he wasn't placed in a box. After meeting with him, and trying to understand his perspective, we were able to hypothesise that this young black male was vulnerable due to his learning needs and easily drawn into gang activity due to isolation from his family. He was able to recognise that he wanted a lifestyle different from his past and he shared his hopes for the future. Although he has had, and will continue to have, challenges along the way, his story from the unit's perspective is not saturated in the difficulties of his past but of a young person with unique strengths.

Ideas of curiosity, hypothesising, circularity are those that have been the easiest to share and are those that we have attempted to implement within unit meetings. It is important not to get caught up in tightly written scripts already made by previous workers. Often negative stories have already been created in previous assessments that maintain the young person's story as problem-saturated, pathologising them as 'non-engaging', 'angry' or having 'problems with authority'. Therefore, we have been keen to test out information and to think about the person's own GRRAACCEESS before we make any assessments or judgements.

In another example, a young person was being transferred to us and the file told of a tremendously difficult care history. A member of the unit reviewed the case file and was hesitant even to begin work with this young person. The file read of physical and verbal abuse towards residential staff including social workers, temper tantrums, arrests, exclusions and evictions. The hesitations the worker experienced were completely understandable. However, she was aware that she would not be working on this case alone, and there was a variety of skills sets in the unit that may be helpful. We discussed the documented case history versus the young person's story, the progress the young person appeared to be making and the value of curiosity when meeting with the young person. The impression the worker gained after a first meeting with the young person was of the potential of working with the young person and viewing her as feisty, with a strong voice and good self-advocacy skills. Of course there will be challenges to escort this vibrant young female through her leaving care experience, but a starting point is seeing the young person as a strong self-advocate rather than impossible to work with, stroppy or difficult. These experiences of reading the file versus knowing the young person cause reflection on the type of documentation that is used in practice. The difficulties and challenges of a young person need to be represented in the file, but documented in a way that does not limit recordings to the problems in a young person's life, but notes their successes and hopes for the future.

The unit model and the systemic lens through which we now view young people invites us to think about and communicate with young people differently. We are now testing hypotheses in a secure environment, identifying repeated scripts (particularly through the use of genograms) and trying to place these in a more positive frame. We are more conscious of identifying strengths and utilising strengths-based language when talking to and about young people, placing all young people's behaviour firmly within their own contexts and interconnected to their individual belief system. Those who are trained and training in systemic practice are sharing this way of thinking with others. It is enriching to see workers who have been, for many years, fixed in a traditional style of working now starting to make shifts to think more relationally and becoming curious. One example is when a worker asked, 'What is happening in my relationship with this young person that does not work for them?' This identifies a shift away from ideas about how young people 'are', but rather beginning to understand their behaviour within a relational context and endeavouring to think about the meaning we are making within the relationship created. Consequently, the approach with a young person not attending college becomes more supportive and meaningful to them, asking questions such as 'What can I do to help support you with the college issue?'

It is curiosity which enables social workers to start to change narratives, to deepen more supportive relationships and influence other professionals' and family members' perceptions. Using tools such as Bateson's GRRAACCEESS model and Pearce's coordinated management of meaning's atomic and hierarchical models have gone some way to helping us develop a deeper understanding of why young may people behave the way they do. Coordinated management of meaning is a heuristic model that guides inquiry and interventions around the relationship construction between meaning and action (Pearce 2007). It is a toolkit that provides context markers, perspectives, angles or stories to aid understanding of 'what goes on' in communication and our place within it. Therefore, it facilitates the questions such as 'Who am I in this?' and 'What's my position?' (Holmgren 2004). Patterns of communication can often reflect good/bad or right/wrong perceptions which can be unhelpful in moving dialogue forward. This way of thinking can become embedded as stories in organisational culture, relationships and identities. This model provides tools such to be used to examine communication, seek explanations, develop questions linked to hypothesis and therefore helps more effective dialogue. Using these models facilitates a more collaborative rather than oppositional stance from workers. It is through collaboration that we hope we can give young people the opportunity to learn from their own experiences. Considering behaviour within their own context allows us to have a more curious dialogue with the young person (rather than what can be sometimes seen as two monologues). We are hopeful that this will facilitate their opportunity to reflect and connect behaviour to their own value base and thus make choices to bring about changes that fit for them. This is often the only time changes will stick.

In order to try to develop a context where we hypothesise about our young people we are endeavouring to ask circular questions while in unit meetings. Cecchin (1987) proposed using 'if' questions in order to try to ascertain patterns rather than facts. Additionally, Hedges (2005) highlights that genograms 'become an important way of joining and a way of showing the interconnectedness of relationships with families' (p.85). This is helping to explore the relationships between people, future, present and past. The Milan Team, which highly influenced early systemic thoughts, advised replacing the verb 'to be' with the verb 'to show' (Cecchin 1987). One way to use this idea is through asking questions such as 'How is he showing he's angry?', 'Who else notices he's angry?', 'How does his mother experience his anger?' These tools enable us to try to really understand what is happening for a young person.

For Karen, working within the unit style and developing systemic practice facilitated a 'eureka' moment within her social work practice. Despite over ten years' experience and considering herself as a sound practitioner, she had never purposefully and regularly shared hypotheses or hunches with young people as to why they may be behaving the way they did. This sounds so obvious and makes her feel a little incredulous now. However, working in this more transparent manner demonstrates a more respectful and helpful dialogue. While working with a young white male care leaver living in a semi-independent unit, suspected of dealing drugs for older gang members, demonstrating minimal self-care skills and failing to engage with residential staff, the hypothesis was shared that he was searching for a sense of belonging and self-worth from negative peers due to feeling disconnected from his birth family. He stated that he thought that was not correct, and we moved on within our discussion. However, the following week he told a residential worker that he felt unloved and unwanted by his mother and didn't feel as valued as his siblings. This was a major breakthrough with this young person who had been very keen to maintain an image of a 'tough guy'. Our focus with the young person became to try to connect him to his family network, or, as this proved to be fruitless at that point, to focus on work on supporting him to try to develop his resilience, resources and support networks elsewhere. Workers usually have two or three ideas about why a young person may be doing what they are doing, and it is often useful to share all of them with the young person to give the message that multiple possibilities exist and co-exist. This way we open up the possibility that the young person may come forward with one or two hypotheses of their own.

Relationships with systems

Not only are we aiming to help co-construct more helpful narratives with the young people about themselves and their previous experiences through our relationships with them, but we are also aiming to re-author how young people are perceived by integral partner agencies which provide day-to-day support. Our aim is to ensure they can develop more helpful collaborative relationships with these supports, as well as with us. Influencing the system around the young person is vital if the young person is to feel supported and to move forward positively. While working with an 18-year-old black African Caribbean care leaver recently released from prison, we were hearing narratives from keyworkers that he was unwilling to engage or receive any support or guidance and, due to his resistance and lack of communication, they suspected he would re-offend and be recalled to custody. These ideas around the young person do not prove helpful to connect with the young person and develop a respectful relationship where the young person feels valued. With the unit's therapist (via consistent attempts to engage with him over the phone) he began to talk about feeling the need to get things done but being at a loss of what to do, feeling overwhelmed and feelings of paranoia getting in the way of him proceeding with what needed to be done and working with others. Now, instead of the story being one of a young person unwilling to engage with professionals and possibly re-offending, it may potentially become one of him unsure about how to adjust to life coming out of prison. The focus can now shift to liaising with the system around him, to put his apparent disinterest in the context of uncertainty and readjustment rather than to do with his attitude or behaviour. The aim is to elicit different responses from those around him to create an opportunity to deepen relationships with people who are willing to be responsive. This may well lay excellent foundations for more focused work to be done with him about reducing the feelings of paranoia.

The ideas about re-writing narratives are not limited to the view of social services towards a young person, but also helping the young person and their family to think about the dominant discourse and if there are other ways their story could be told. One young person, Abdur, comes from a family that migrated to London from Nigeria when he was about five years old. Several child protection referrals were made while at school which were closed after an initial assessment. When he was 14, he stole a mobile phone and was caught. Upon stating that the school would call his family, Abdur started to cry and said his parents would beat him up if they found out. Following the investigation, Abdur has been in care and has very limited contact with his family, which could be perceived as Abdur's choice. Now at age 16, he is involved in gang activity and puts himself at risk through not following curfews and carrying weapons.

When beginning to work with this case, the dominant voices sounded could be interpreted as below.

> Abdur's voice: 'I hate social services. Nobody does their job properly and everyone keeps telling me to go home. I do not have to listen to you and can do what I want.'

> School's voice: 'Abdur is destined either to kill or be killed. He comes from a good family and his behaviour has deteriorated since going into care.'

> Mother's voice: 'Abdur is your responsibility now.'

> Foster carer's voice: 'Abdur does not listen and does what he wants.'

> Social services' voice: 'We need to do everything we can to keep Abdur safe.'

Working systemically involves keeping an open mind to different points of view, especially from colleagues and systemic practitioners. This case was discussed in depth in unit meetings, but there was also the possibility to discuss the case with colleagues at systemic course days and in systemic practice groups. A multitude of suggestions were available on how to understand the context of the case, ideas around how to work with Abdur and his family, the pace that may be best for Abdur, developing relationships with a young adolescent male, ideas around cultural identity, and for Abdur, what it means to be male, as well as a hypothesis that Abdur needed to know that we would stick by him and not give up, as he does not trust easily. These conversations also yielded a profound sense of hope, that the work being done was highly valuable, and although it would be challenging, it would bring about change. From listening to the multitude of voices and having further discussions with all members, a few potential hypotheses were developed. These were all held lightly and gently tested to see if they would fit with Abdur and his family.

1. Abdur misses his family. He asks about them regularly and a look of profound sadness crosses his face when they are mentioned. He knows where his family lives and how to contact them, but has not done so. He appears not to know how to reach out to them. He feels alone, and reaches out to friends and protectors in local gangs.

2. Abdur's parents are angry with Abdur and with social services. They were unfamiliar with how social services was run and feel powerless to help their son. They are very concerned and worried about Abdur but do not know what to do.

3. Abdur has learned that he has control over his own life. He has the power to make his own decisions and will not be easily swayed by inflicting rules and boundaries.

In working with this case, one piece of work that Abdur was asking for was to be reunited with his family. This involved some in-depth conversations with Abdur's parents, who at first wanted nothing to do with social workers. They appeared to feel that they had had many meetings with social workers in the past, which had been unhelpful. After many attempts at conversations, messages left and unreturned phone calls, a breakthrough happened when Abdur's mother unleashed her anger by describing how she really felt about Abdur being taken into care, her concern about him running wild on the streets and her perception that she was seen as a bad parent. She said Abdur could contact her if he wanted, but she wanted no meetings with social workers. Further conversations, including using reflective questioning techniques, revealed how concerned they were about Abdur, how much they loved him and cared about him. This re-framing of anger to concern was key to Abdur's parents' understanding that we had a similar perspective of concern for Abdur, and for them being more open to working with social workers and the starting point of having a relationship with Abdur. The question of 'How can we help Abdur see how much you care about him?' started new dialogue and understanding. Although at a starting point, the rehabilitation means that Abdur is slowly seeing that his parents care about him.

Patterns in relationships

There are many systemic techniques that can be used to try to understand communication and patterns within the multitude of relationships. Systemic practice also requires a continuous high level of self-reflection and looking at the role of practitioner and the patterns that develop with clients. As previously mentioned, the idea of 'What can I be doing differently?' helps the worker reflect on their individual role within the relationship and what can be done differently to influence change. One idea, from Pearce's coordinated management of meaning model (Pearce 2007), looks at communication patterns with practitioners and clients and analyses these patterns. Sometimes a pattern may develop called a strange loop that heeds any progress as the communication goes in a continuous cycle. A simplified example follows, in Figure 8.1.

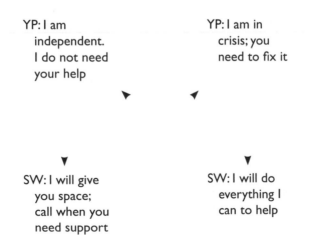

Figure 8.1 An example of a strange loop

In situations such as these, the social worker is as much a part of the pattern as the young person. According to this model, if one part of the pattern changes, by consequence the other part will also have to change. It only remains the same as long as both participants keep the same lines of communication. This helps the practitioner think about what can be done differently to illicit change in particular situations. By thinking as a unit to identify and change patterns of engagement between practitioners and young people, we can be creative and think of new methods and techniques to move the young person forward.

Conclusion

Working systemically has made social work feel different from our previous experiences in social work practice. We have highlighted how working systemically allows us to consider carefully the importance of relationships in our social work involvement. Thinking systemically is not only consideration of the young person and the different relationships in their environment. By drawing on systemic theory, we are able to consider carefully the relationships we have with young people and the influence of our relationship in a creative and flexible way. In our units, we are able to think about what may be most useful to the young person, form hypotheses about complex situations and plan interventions. As consultant social workers, learning about systemic theory and applying these techniques to daily practice has been a journey that has challenged us to think differently about the relationships we form with young people and how our relationship is a tool to help move young people forward.

Commentary by David and Yvonne Shemmings

Most readers will have noticed a resurgence of the importance of the 'relationship' in social work; it has even acquired its own soubriquet: *relationship-based social work*. But the term means far more than the essentially tautological idea that 'social workers need to have a relationship with service users': that is obvious and applies equally well to doctors, teachers and health visitors. In fact, it applies to virtually everyone who works with people. To think and talk about social work as needing to be 'relationship-based' connotes the sense that *relationships themselves* are the central focus of assessment, reflection and intervention. *Relationship-based social work* involves being endlessly *curious* – that word again – about a person's mind when they encounter another human being, be it their child, their partner, or, of course, the social worker. To such relational encounters we each bring our childhood biographies, our successes and failures in the past, and our hopes and fears for the future…but reciprocated *meaning* is found not so much within each individual, but more in the 'space between us' (Josselson 1996). In that sense, *relationship-based social work* emphasises the psychosocial over the exclusively psychological. With that in mind, we thought the idea of replacing the verb 'to be' with the verb 'to show' – asking questions such as 'How is he showing he is angry?', Who else notices he's angry?' 'How does his mother experience his anger?' – was an excellent way to deliberately shake up and intentionally problematise that relationship by forcing us to allow the 'known to become unknown'. Doing this means we are less likely to pigeonhole family members, and the example illustrates neatly how Hackney Reclaiming Social Work is bringing theory and research into social work practice.

Donald Forrester has recently completed research to find out how social workers communicate with family members, especially those who are reluctant or resistant (Forrester and Harwin 2008). He and his colleagues developed a creative design involving two social workers who enacted two different child protection scenarios. Both were 'typical' referrals but one contained more problematic and 'serious' concerns than the other. Twenty-four social workers were then asked to respond to the two 'actors' as they would in practice. Each vignette concerned parental substance misuse amidst the care of a young person. The 'actors' were not given a fixed script; instead, they were encouraged to use what might be termed a 'Mike Leigh' approach:[1] the 'actors' were given an overall direction for the scenario, along with some basic information about the referral, but over and above that they were asked to respond as 'naturally' as possible to the social workers. So if the social worker dealt sensitively with the 'actor' as the interview unfolded, then they would 'reward' such practice with more disclosure and/or increased cooperation. The advantage of using simulated scenarios is that, in the main, each subject is responding to the 'same' situation, hence comparisons are possible in ways which would be more difficult if actual family members in 'real' scenarios were studied. Analysing interviews with family members

---

1   Mike Leigh is a notable British film director who has won awards for numerous works including *Secrets and Lies*.

increases authenticity but it reduces the potential for contrasts to be made between workers.

Donald Forrester found that although the practitioners were quite good at expressing the concerns raised in the referral information, they showed far less empathy than would have been expected. This is worrying, given that it is clear that practitioners who demonstrate empathy significantly increase the level of trust, disclosure and cooperation shown by family members, provided it is blended with a down-to-earth, streetwise nous laced with an implacable ability not to have the wool pulled over their eyes. In fact, it can be reasonably assumed that a family member who does not respond to accurate empathy in this way really *is* resistant.

Also, practitioners studied did not display good listening skills, preferring instead to ask lots of closed questions as opposed to open ones (despite their qualification training almost certainly having stressed the latter over the former). Additionally, they used few reflections in the interviews and there were almost no references to positives. We stressed earlier what we see as some of the problems in espousing a naive version of a 'strengths-based' approach, but we were shocked to find in Donald Forrester's study a strange confection of rather harsh, bureaucratic and impersonal approaches to child protection investigation. At one level, for this group of practitioners at any rate, it appears at first sight as though the pioneering work of Carl Rogers, Robert Carkhuff and Gerard Egan had been thrown out of the window; but perhaps we were seeing a reaction to what some social workers may see as the naiveté of applying communication skills used by counsellors. Although they almost certainly will have encountered 'communication skills' on their qualifying programme, perhaps social workers now view their use as fine for a therapist in her consulting room, working with 'clients' who attend the weekly 'therapeutic hour' of their own free will, but as having little relevance to a reluctant family member high on coke and hell-bent on duping rookie child protection practitioners – so argues the 21st-century, street-wise, burned-out, media-pilloried social worker.

We believe such a position is far too cynical, and we are impressed by the degree to which it is implicitly challenged by Hackney Reclaiming Social Work. We believe there is a serious problem when the Rogerian core conditions of empathy, respect and warmth are seen as 'soft', especially if they are perceived as an alternative to a 'tell it to them straight', no-nonsense stance which may be adopted uncritically by some practitioners to deal with, as they see it, the modern-day, falsely compliant, uncooperative or outright aggressive parent. But it is precisely such a parent who will react badly to an insensitive 'tell it like it is' caustic attitude. We need to remember that social workers actually have very few powers when they don't have clear evidence that a child is at risk of maltreatment; any attempt on their part to throw their weight about is likely to become dangerously unstuck. By combining sensitivity with realism and compassion for the parent with a fierce and urgent need to protect a child when necessary, the Hackney Reclaiming Social Work project closes the gap between inappropriately positioned binary opposites. Anchoring 'compassion and sensitivity' at one end of a spectrum with 'toughness and incisiveness' at the other is as unwarranted as it is misplaced.

With some notable and notorious exceptions, such as Rosemary and Frederick West,[2] we have always believed that the majority of parents who abuse their children *would prefer not to*. It is also the case that maltreating parents are very likely to have neurological 'gaps' and biochemical imbalances which account for the attributional errors and low mentalisation that are the precursors for – and accompany – much abuse. This doesn't mean that abusing parents 'can't help it' or that they have no responsibility for what they do. But they can't make the changes on their own. They need, and often want, help; but they rarely admit it. One of the best placed professionals to give such help is a social worker. But an outstretched hand of assistance to a parent later on in the relationship is likely to be bitten off if, during the early stages when allegations were investigated, the social worker acted like an insensitive, overbearing council official.

References

Bateson, G. (1978) *Steps to an Ecology of Mind.* London: Paladin Books.

Burnham, J. (1986) *Family Therapy.* London: Tavistock.

Cecchin, G. (1987) 'Hypothesising, circularity and neutrality revisited: an invitation to curiosity.' *Family Process 26,* 4, 405–413.

Dallos, R. and Draper, R. (2005) *An Introduction to Family Therapy.* Buckingham: Open University Press.

Forrester, D. and Harwin, J. (2008) 'Parental substance misuse and child welfare: Outcomes for children two years after referral.' *British Journal of Social Work 38,* 8, 1518–1535.

---

2   Notorious serial killers who abused, tortured and murdered a number of children, including some of their own.

Hedges, F. (2005) *An Introduction to Systemic Therapy with Individuals*. Basingstoke: Palgrave Macmillan.

Holmgren, A. (2004) 'Saying, doing and making: teaching CMM theory.' *Human Systems* *15*, 2, 89–100.

Jones, E. (1993) *Family Therapy: Developments in the Milan-Systemic Therapies*. Chichester: Wiley.

Josselson, R. (1996) *The Space Between Us: Exploring the Dimensions of Human Relationships*. Thousand Oaks, CA: Sage.

Pearce, W.B. (2007) *Making Social Worlds*. Oxford: Blackwell Publishing.

Young, J., Saunders, F., Prentice, G., Macri-Riseley, D., Fitch, R. and Pati-Tasca, C. (1997) 'Three journeys toward the reflecting team.' *Australia and New Zealand Journal of Family Therapy 18*, 1, 27–37.

CHAPTER 9

Liberated Thinking within a Social Work Unit

Rick Mason

I became a consultant social worker in one of the new social work units in Hackney in 2008, having worked previously for many years as a social worker in the borough. The unit works with up to 45 looked-after children with a long-term care plan other than adoption, meaning we mainly work with older children/teenagers and their families and networks. The social worker, clinician, children's practitioner and unit coordinator working with me have shared my commitment and enthusiasm for this project. I am very grateful for their support and hard work in helping to put Reclaiming Social Work into practice.

In this chapter, I consider how our thinking has been liberated in the unit, both through the new structure and an explicit systemic approach. I then look through some anonymised case examples, at how this thinking has impacted on social work practice in the unit. What I mean by thinking, in this social work context at least, is the process of making meanings. This is a systemic and social constructionist position. All of the young people we work with in the unit have highly complex histories, many characterised by trauma, separation and loss. How we think about these multiple stories leads to what questions we ask, or how we refine these meanings, and subsequently, to what we do. If this thinking is more open, curious, creative – able to hold positions from different viewpoints – then the social work engagement that follows leads to more positive ways forward for those we work with. Both the way that social workers (and others) are organised to work together, and the approaches and perspectives they bring to this, are critical to the extent to which such open thinking is possible.

Organisational structure

In the 'traditional' statutory social work model, a social work team consists of a team manager, about seven social workers and an administrator. In a team working with looked-after children, each social worker might hold on average 14 cases. The manager offers case management and support, mainly through monthly supervision meetings. This is the principal opportunity in this structure for social work thinking and reflection. Social workers offer a basic 'cover' service for each other's cases in emergencies, with little sharing of the work, or the thinking, beyond this. The manager rarely becomes involved directly in casework, and would often themselves be overwhelmed by the sheer number of cases, levels of stress, and their bureaucratic and human resources management responsibilities. In my long experience of this traditional model, weekly team meetings were, at best, policy and process led, and a dumping ground for feelings. The social worker then is largely reliant on their relationship with their overstretched manager for thinking about their cases in this model.

This very limited opportunity to think about the work, and then to share some responsibility about the strategies adopted, is in my view a key component of the high stress levels and burn-out which have bedevilled social work. This stress tends to make it harder still to separate our thinking from what we are going to do, closing down our thinking still further. Perhaps this 'privatising' of casework, if you will, has been driven by a requirement for accountability, but time and again even this does not seem to hold. It feels as if nearly every inquiry into social work system failure cites a lack of structural clarity about professional responsibilities. This casework isolation and restricted thinking is a context for a blame culture. A familiar story might go that the manager had too many cases to oversee and could only respond to what the social worker brought to them, while the social worker was inexperienced at such complex and demanding work, overstretched, and left on their own to worry about their cases. This traditional configuration of a social work team should then be seen as an insecure base from which to think about our work. It provides a context for reactive, ill-considered and inconsistent social work that can feel like offering little more than commentaries on doomed lives. Of course, many social workers have risen above this, but this has been against the odds.

The new unit structure offers a smaller, more collaborative and team-based approach, which has reduced the stress levels of staff and allowed us to think in a more open way about the very complex lives and relationships with whom we work. The smaller size of the unit means that all the staff become familiar with all the children held in the unit. Although all the young people served by the unit are formally allocated to me as the consultant social worker, they are given a lead worker from the unit, which could be me, in recognition of the centrality of this relationship in helping young people to feel supported in building their lives. However, whether I am the lead with any particular child or not, I am aware of each child's situation and I take the responsibility for ensuring the direction of the work. My colleagues and I have all felt more held in this role by the unit – by our thinking together about the work and our relationships in it.

The weekly unit meetings have been central to this group reflexivity. The focus of these meetings is discussions about the child, with the aim of discussing each young person in as much detail as is required. We have agreed a process for each case discussion in my unit, as follows:

1. Update of developments since last discussion – some preparation is needed.

2. Our feelings about this – allowing a focus on the optimistic and positive as well as the fears and frustrations.

3. Our thinking – the lead worker is encouraged to bring any dilemmas about their work to the meeting, and all the staff reflect and hypothesise about the work and the social work/ therapeutic relationships involved in each case.

4. Plans – it has been surprisingly difficult to keep the practical decision-making separate from our reflections, but we have got better at this. Finding the space to think collectively without worrying about what we are going to do has shaped better decision-making.

Having a clinician as a member of the unit has promoted and modelled this hypothesising in the unit meetings and encouraged curiosity among the social work staff. The clinician has also been able to be much more responsive to the therapeutic needs of the children, without the need for referral and so on, and to work (and think) jointly with social work staff.

The unit coordinator is much more able than the old team administrators to undertake paperwork and practical tasks for the social work staff, given the smaller size of the unit. This has freed up much more time in the unit for direct work. The longer-term aim of streamlining the requirements of social work reports has also begun, with young people's social work review minutes now incorporating the child's care plan, obviating the need for separate, and often duplicating, documents. The unit coordinator also formally minutes the unit meeting discussions, which are placed on the young people's social work files.

My consultant social worker role is very different from that of the old team manager, in that my job remains rooted in practice. The previous career structure encouraged progression into non-practitioner/management roles, removing from the front-line social work service many skilled and experienced practitioners. This change has been possible because all human resources issues are managed separately, by the group manager. This means that the consultant social worker role is much more of a leadership than management one, still embedded in direct work, and more able to share skills and experience. This is a less hierarchical and more collaborative model – although I am accountable for all the work in the unit, this responsibility feels much more shared in the unit through our joint working and thinking.

I provide monthly supervision to the social worker and children's practitioner (with the clinician and unit coordinator separately supervised by specialists in their area of expertise). These supervision sessions focus on the feelings raised by the work, and training needs/discussions. Case discussions are not held at these times – rather, they centre on the worker themselves, providing space for personal reflection and promoting their resilience and professional development.

Approaches and perspectives

Social work in practice in the UK currently has a good value base, but is an eclectic and sometimes contradictory mix of ill thought out and rarely understood systemic and psycho-dynamic approaches, which have not offered practitioners a secure enough base or framework for their thinking. Nevertheless, systemic ideas are implicit in the paperwork systems prescribed to us – for example, in the nationally prescribed paperwork for looked-after children (DfES 2004). It has been suggested to me that all the extensive forms that social workers are required to complete were introduced to compensate for the low skills base in the profession. If true, then this has only made matters worse, as social workers have become ever more tied to paper processes, reducing our contact with young people and families, and delimiting our potential for curiosity. This leads to more knee-jerk responses from social workers. When managing risk, for example, a lack of curiosity and open thinking leads to more defensive and confrontational practice. Systemic practice cannot be introduced by stealth, as it were, but needs to be employed explicitly, with curiosity at its heart. Hackney is the first social work department in the UK to announce that it is adopting a systemic approach, and planning its provision accordingly. This has been an exciting journey. For me and my social work colleagues in the unit, it is perhaps the hitherto implicit systemic underpinning of social work that has made adopting an explicit systemic approach feel like such a good fit.

Developing systemic thinking and techniques within the unit has been strongly supported by the unit clinician, with other staff being given professional training as systemic practitioners (lasting two years). Much of this thinking is now shared within the unit, to provide frameworks for our thinking about casework. The coordinated management of meaning (Pearce 2007) offers a hierarchy of contexts of meaning, with culture being the highest context. This has been a helpful framework for thinking about different cultural perspectives within the unit, which is a mixed group, and with families from a very diverse range of backgrounds. Gender and class contexts are also important in how we make meanings – ideas about identity are implicit within these different social and political contexts. We consider our positioning as practitioners with young people and families, often choosing non-expert positions and more playful approaches. Ideas from narrative therapy and attachment narrative therapy have been particularly helpful when thinking about this positioning, and in looking to co-construct meanings with young people with whom we are working long term. Thinking about attachment, always seen as central in work with looked-after children, has evolved from a more pathologising psycho-dynamic position to ways of thinking about different patterns of attachment behaviour – a more hopeful position.

This more developed systemic thinking has engendered development in our social work techniques, including circular and reflexive questioning, use of family network meetings, genogram work, role-play, timeline and refined life-story book work, therapeutic letters and the use of externalisation techniques. Indeed, there can seem to be little separating the social work and clinical staff in the unit in terms of their perspectives or even techniques, although the clinician is able to benefit the unit's thinking by sharing their greater expertise.

There is much written about the importance of engagement and the therapeutic relationship in achieving therapeutic change. The importance of engagement and the social work relationship with service users is also widely recognised in social work, although not effectively in policy terms – looked-after young people have often complained about the high turnover of their social workers. The unit model does offer greater continuity in this. It is through feeling held and secure in key relationships that young people can develop and mature to their potential, and in the way they want. The relationship with the social worker, as with the clinician, is particularly important in this for looked-after young people. Systemic thinking helps us to understand this and to think about and prioritise these relationships, which necessarily involve time. We have reflected during unit meetings on the minutiae of interactions in these relationships when we have felt stuck in them, as well as reflecting on our positioning in this.

Some case examples from the unit

I now give some anonymised examples of casework within the unit which I have led on, which illustrates how more open thinking has happened in the unit, and the positive consequences this has brought in terms of changing the stories of young people.

1. Chloe

Chloe is a 15-year-old of dual heritage. Her white British mother, Shirley (age 40), has a long-standing diagnosis of chronic mental health problems (schizophrenia), which resulted, due to neglect, in Chloe becoming looked-after subject to a care order, aged five, along with her half-brothers, George (then aged 11) and Barry (then aged nine). They had lived together with a local foster family for two years when the foster father committed suicide. In the confusion which followed this traumatic event, Chloe had returned to her mother's care with her brothers being found alternative placements. Over the next five years Chloe had remained with her mother, with some monitoring by social workers. She would stay with her grandfather, Rolf (age 70), locally when her mother was hospitalised, but generally her mother was supported in the community by the mental health service. Chloe's father, Raymond (age 30), is of mixed white UK/African-Caribbean heritage. He has a history of drug dealing and violent offending, and is currently serving a long prison term. He has had little of a parenting role with Chloe, although members of his family have maintained some contact with her independently of social workers, and against her mother's wishes. He was only 15 when Chloe was born.

The unit started to work with Chloe when she was 13. The physical standards within the home were poor, with Chloe experiencing little consistent parenting and acting as a child carer in many ways for her mother. Her school attendance and presentation were both good, however, and she had lots of friends and was performing at an average academic level. We were uncomfortable as a unit about the resilience of this arrangement, but there was clearly a loving attachment between Chloe and her mother, who both very much wanted to stay together, and support for this among Shirley's extended family. We resolved to try to support this arrangement through me building relationships with Chloe, Shirley, Rolf, George, Barry and others in the network. Over the next year Chloe's behaviour became much less contained, more risky and problematic. She increasingly became involved in fights and truancy in school, and also in falling out with her mother and not respecting boundaries at home. From unit discussion about this, the clinician became involved with Chloe and others in the network. My role became increasingly to establish, support and challenge around boundaries for Chloe at home and in school, while the clinician took a co-authoring position with Chloe, to help her to think about the difficulties she was facing. After some months of balancing the risks inherent in this strategy, Chloe had agreed to being placed in foster care. This was a big step, as Chloe had previously threatened to burn down any foster home she was sent to. This, I think, showed the value of our approach, of giving her a sense of being held – through my boundary setting, chasing up and networking (a parental position) and the clinician's complementary encouragement, re-framings and co-reflexivity. Perhaps her decision that she needed to be fostered was also influenced by some of the dangers she had encountered. Although she settled well with the African-Caribbean foster family, who interested her culturally, she continued to see her old friends, and within two months she was arrested in relation to a serious gang-related assault, and then discovered that she was pregnant (aged 14) by the gang leader (aged 15).

This was a critical moment for Chloe. Both the clinician and I felt the unit meeting discussions about Chloe at this point helped us to feel held in our work, and our thinking as a unit remained open after we had acknowledged our feelings. I wrote a long therapeutic letter to Chloe, with the help of the unit, about the difficult choice she had to make regarding whether to continue with her pregnancy. This essentially re-framed her 'challenging' and 'wilful' behaviour as *her determination*. This appeared to have a profound impact on Chloe when I first read her the letter, and continues to resonate for her. I think she might have read that letter a hundred times. This engaged her in the question, 'Who am I, and who do I want to be?'

Chloe decided to go ahead with her pregnancy, and with continued therapeutic support she focused on, and planned for, the birth, engaging well with all the support offered. I supported her through the criminal prosecution, with the charges against her eventually being dropped. I also assessed a step maternal aunt in Kent as carer for Chloe and the baby, where she moved before her daughter's birth, in line with her wishes. This possibility perhaps only arose thanks to the trusting relationships we had built over time within the family.

Chloe and baby are both now doing well. Chloe has shown a confidence and maturity far beyond her years in adapting to motherhood. She is attending school, where she is described as a model pupil, and plans to go on to further education. She has developed a close and supportive relationship with her step aunt, who was also a teenage mother. She maintains wider family contact, but has taken a step back from her former friendship group, including her former boyfriend. Although our work with Chloe is ongoing, our approach has harnessed her resilience through holding her in her relationships with us (and others), such that she could find a secure space to think of solutions to her own problems. With these ongoing relationships it is likely, I think, to be easier for her to overcome future difficulties.

2. Dean

Dean is a 13-year-old of African-Caribbean heritage. He has been looked-after, since the age of two, subject to a care order. His parents, who are separated but still friends, both have learning difficulties, and were assessed as being unable to stimulate him adequately or keep him safe. Dean, aged two, was placed in foster care with an older African-Caribbean couple, with several older foster children, on a short-term basis, until he could be placed for adoption. This was never achieved. One attempt broke down at an early stage.

Dean was then moved, aged eight, to a younger, African-Caribbean long-term foster family: Clara, Edwin and their four children. Within a few months he had alleged physical abuse against his former foster mother (which was never proven), although he did still miss her. It has become apparent that there was little emotional warmth available to Dean in the rigid home life of this foster placement. Several contact meetings were arranged for Dean with his parents each year (he had no other family contacts), but these offered a very limited emotional dimension.

Dean found it difficult to concentrate in school from the start, falling behind academically, and regularly getting into fights. Good support from his primary school had helped him to manage his behaviour better, and to make some academic progress. These staff, however, had been concerned by his blank expressions and apparent emotional withdrawal.

Dean managed the transition to his long-term foster home quite well, forming a good friendship with the carers' son (one year his junior), with whom he chose to share a room. His behaviour in his new school was less contained initially, but again responded well to good mentoring and teaching assistant support. However, his continued blank expressions and apparent emotional withdrawal raised concern in the new school, and with Clara and Edwin.

Dean was allocated to the unit aged ten, 18 months after this placement move. Although he appeared to be settled and progressing, Clara and Edwin were very concerned about his emotional withdrawal, and were worried that he was bullying their son, although the two boys appeared to have a good friendship. Their view was that he was a 'damaged child', who was 'not normal' and needed intensive therapy. We thought together in the unit meeting about this position. We agreed that this position reflected a pathologising story that had developed about Dean in the previous professional network, which was still maintained by the foster carers' supervising social worker. We sought to re-write this story along the lines that Dean had had limited emotional experiences in his relationships with previous attachment figures, which made it very difficult for him to articulate or make sense of his feelings. His avoidant pattern of behaviours was understandable as a response to this. What he needed in this was to learn about engagement in such emotional life as part of an understanding and nurturing family.

We met as a unit with the supervising social worker to discuss these positions, and I also met with Clara and Edwin several times to discuss this, and to encourage them to see that the changes they wanted in Dean's emotional engagement would be achieved in time with their understanding, loving care. I got quite stuck in this work, with Clara and Edwin insisting that Dean was bullying their son, and insisting that he be seen by a therapist. After further unit discussion the unit clinician then undertook this assessment, which focused as much on Clara and Edwin as on Dean. This was uncomfortable for them, and perhaps touched their sensitivity for being blamed for Dean's quite cold effect. The clinician provided Clara and Edwin with her written report. This acted rather like a therapeutic letter for them, with the focus on their many qualities as excellent foster carers, and on Dean's resilience and survival through his emotionally deprived earlier life experience, and had a major impact on them both. They withdrew from the supervising social worker, who resisted the unit's position, and quickly showed much greater confidence and enthusiasm in their fostering role. There appears to have been no basis to the bullying concerns, which the carers now understand as normal sibling rivalries. This bullying issue is a good example of how the 'logical force' of stories or beliefs can develop.

Since this time, Dean has progressed very well in secondary school, where he now excels in sport, continues to catch up academically with a positive attitude to learning and where there are no concerns about his behaviour. Dean is very settled as part of his foster family, with Clara and Edwin both demonstrably very proud of him. He has gradually become more emotionally engaged, which they have appreciated. He continues to see his parents several times each year, in line with his wishes, but Clara has taken over managing this from me. Clara and Edwin have now made a special guardianship order application regarding Dean, with his support, and the backing of my department and his parents.

3. Charity

Charity is a 13-year-old of African heritage. She came to England with her father in 2002, leaving her mother and two younger sisters in Mozambique. They had planned to join them later. In 2005 Charity alleged sexual abuse against her father, who was convicted and sentenced to four years' imprisonment. Charity was at this point placed by social workers, with minimal checks, with her maternal aunt Adeline and uncle João. Within six months, Charity (aged nine) and the family's youngest daughter Ruth (aged seven) had alleged that Ruth's brother Ricardo (aged 12, with Down's Syndrome) had sexually abused them. Both girls were accommodated in the same foster placement with the reluctant agreement of Adeline and João. Ricardo was also subsequently accommodated. There were concerns about neglect and the possible sexual abuse of Ricardo, who had very sexualised and sometimes menacing behaviour. Adeline and João attended two separate parenting programmes, and a parenting assessment, but the decision about whether to return Charity to their care stalled.

At this point Charity (and Ruth) were allocated to the unit. They had both lived in their foster placement for 18 months at this point, and both wanted, with increasingly limited patience, to return to Adeline and João's care. We thought about this in the unit meeting. The family had been re-housed to better quality accommodation, and previous concerns about alcohol misuse (by João) were no longer evident. Adeline and João had engaged well in their parenting classes and assessment, although there was still no clarity as to who might have abused Ricardo. We considered contexts for previous professional concerns about the family, including the family's migration to the UK as political refugees ten years earlier, with the loss of status, employment, family and culture that this entailed; their cultural beliefs about parenting and learning difficulties; their history of bereavement and ill-health; and their leading status in their own community in London.

We considered in the unit meeting how we might best manage risk to enable Charity and Ruth both to return home. We convened several family network meetings and developed a good working relationship with their church, of which they were active members. A plan was developed, and within four months both girls had returned to Adeline and João's care, with Charity remaining a looked-after child. In the two years since this time she has made good progress in her aunt and uncle's care. She has a good range of friends and is making progress in school, gradually becoming more self-confident. In line with her wishes she has not been therapeutically engaged, although the unit therapist has co-worked with me with the wider family – she remains willing to work with Charity should she want this, while being mindful of not wanting to undermine Charity's resilience.

There were some concerns for a while about João problem-drinking again. However, he and Adeline did willingly undertake some therapeutic work with me around this problem, using playful externalisation techniques. He found this and his wife's support helpful in being able to stop drinking again. Having these skills in the unit was helpful – João had previously resisted attempts for him to seek help with this problem with professionals unknown to him, and mistrusted.

Charity's father was repatriated to Mozambique after his release from prison, with Charity wanting no contact with him. Her mother has remarried in Mozambique and has given up on trying to move to

England. She has maintained regular telephone contact with Charity. She does not want Charity to return to her care in Mozambique for fear that her father will track her down and 'punish' her for testifying against him. I, with the support of the unit, have worked with Adeline and João to develop a permanency plan for Charity, whereby she will remain in their care subject to a special guardianship order. Charity and her mother both support this plan, and this application is currently before the court.

Final thoughts

I hope these case examples help to illustrate how thinking can be opened up within the new social work unit, and what a difference this can then make. Imagine how the stories of Chloe, Dean and Charity could have developed differently without the unit's thinking. Feeling held in our work by the unit, smaller and more multi-disciplinary than the old team, with much more potential for close professional collaboration, has become a pattern in the unit. This has facilitated our thinking together about highly complex and emotionally charged stories, about calmly managing risk and more self-confidently challenging orthodoxies. The position of the unit clinician in leading the unit in using systemic language and perspectives has provided a rich framework for this thinking.

Commentary by Yvonne Shemmings and David Shemmings

This chapter provides an excellent example of how the Reclaiming model elicits non-reactive case discussion and planning. It also illustrates how the attention paid to unprocessed feelings is aimed at augmenting the quality of the decisions made. It is one of many examples of Hackney Reclaiming Social Work demonstrating how contemporary research findings have contributed to the design of the support offered to workers. This is important because insufficient attention paid to the affective side of the decision-making process seriously impairs its quality. We were also struck by the title of this chapter, because social workers tell us they feel like headless chickens reared on a battery farm, where the space and the time to think is discouraged and replaced by an insistence on the completion of seemingly endless forms containing lots of data but very little information.

The important connection between the 'team' offering practitioners a secure base has also been made in this chapter. Most workers will from time to time use the office as a place of safety, a haven for them to return after having worked with families who they will often feel are resistant or unappreciative (or even both). The office and the 'team' acquire the status of a mothership, to which the intrepid traveller returns after the challenges encountered during the day; not quite a place to put her feet up, more somewhere to refuel and restock. But such an image is only half the story when it comes to thinking about security and safe havens. What the authors also highlight is that the purpose of the safe haven is to act as a secure base from which to feel confident – indeed, 'liberated' – enough to *explore*. The mark of the securely attached child is that they can use their parent as a base from which to find out about the world; initially their toys but, later on, their feelings and thoughts about other people. The chapter presents good examples of how the processes operating in teams not only offer practitioners a bolt-hole, they also encourage and nurture 'critical friend' relationships where individuals can explore and challenge each other's ideas about families. From what we read, they can also rely on the culture engendered in the team to help them make sense of family situations and the dynamics in which they feel 'stuck'.

What also caught our attention was the implied reference to the two meanings of 'supervision'. On the one hand, it means having 'super' (or *better*) 'vision': the ability to see things that others can't, not because they have defective eyesight but as the result of them being too close to the subject, leaving them with a blurred focus. All of us occasionally concentrate on the trees while forgetting that they are part of a wood. We can all, therefore, provide 'super' 'vision' to others, simply because we are not anything like as closely involved. But the idea of 'super' 'vision' also means to 'over' 'see'. The Hackney Reclaiming Social Work project appears to be able to hold practitioners to account for and justify their assessments and actions without becoming excessively 'top-down'; we imagine that this is because the 'overseeing' is often undertaken by team members themselves, rather than by managers alone. The approaches to supervision employed in Hackney Reclaiming Social Work recognise that to expose individuals' practice requires the kind of safe haven and secure base mentioned above.

The concept of hypothesising is mentioned in other chapters, but examples which appear here reinforce its importance. One of the advantages of a hypothesis-based approach emerges in a situation we encountered some years ago. Two girls aged nine are playing on a seesaw in the park. The older sister of the girl at one end overhears the other one say 'I love this game; it's just like going up and down on my willy.'

She phoned social services because she thought it odd. A social worker called on the mother of the girl and explained what had happened. The girl's mother very quickly replied 'Typical social worker, jumping to conclusions; that's the name of her rocking-horse.'

Using a hypothesis-driven approach means actively considering the possibility that this could have been indicative of sexual abuse but at the same time deliberately considering other explanations – the null hypothesis (that is, that it is *not* sexual abuse). The problem when we jump to conclusions is that we are highly likely to take account only of what confirms an inflexibly held viewpoint. Crucially, however, a hypothesis-based approach would also consider the possibility that the mother's reaction was part of a pre-agreed response, because abuse *is* taking place. This does not mean that a social worker should never believe what people say; it is simply a reminder that she needs to have an open mind, but not an empty head.

Finally, we welcomed the inclusive approach to different theories and interventions. While Hackney Reclaiming Social Work draws unashamedly on systemic theory, research and clinical practice, it is also comfortable listening to attachment-based approaches as well as psycho-dynamic ideas from the Tavistock Institute of Human Relations. We have also noticed that previously oppositional approaches to understating human behaviour and interaction – such as attachment-informed therapists and cognitive behaviour therapists – have, at last, started talking to each other. We were pleased, for example, that at a recent one-day conference at the Anna Freud Centre in November 2009, devoted to 'Working with Traumatised Children', cognitive behavioural therapy (CBT) and attachment were linked in a number of expert presentations.[1] Long may such rapprochement last!

References

DfES (2004) *Common Assessment Framework.* London: DfES.
Pearce, W. (2007) *Making Social Worlds: A Communication Perspective.* Oxford: Blackwell.

---

1   At a conference entitled 'Child Abuse: Neuroscience and Intervention'.

CHAPTER 10

Helping People Move Beyond Their Own Histories

Martin Purbrick

Working with families where there is a long-standing involvement with the local authority social services department, often over a number of generations, is a common experience for many social workers. These families, where one generation moves on to the next generation with little change and a repetition of the same dysfunction, can sometimes be the most challenging to work with.

The familiarity with the social work services' repeated interventions can lead to distrust and this is in turn can lead to a relationship between the family and the social worker where there are frequent angry and aggressive outbursts towards the professionals. This can be as a method for the family to maintain some control over what is happening to them or as a way of avoiding the reason for the intervention. Whatever the reason, it is an unpleasant experience for the professionals as it can lead to feelings of fear that they are working in an environment where they are actually in danger of being attacked or coming to some harm.

This in turn can lead to a drop in the quality of the work being undertaken as well as having the effect of diverting the social workers' attention away from the children in the family and leaving them in a dangerous situation.

Using the Reclaiming Social Work model enables the consultant social worker to work in a safe and productive way with the most challenging families. The ability to work safely by visiting in pairs becomes standard practice.

The family

The Phillips family are a large family that have been involved with the social services department for the last two generations which is, in total, over 34 years of intervention. The need for this intervention has been a long and difficult history of alcohol and drug misuse, combined with parental mental health problems, periods of domestic violence and the inability of the parents to understand the effect their behaviour will have on their children and consequently to keep them safe.

Sandra Phillips has had a total of seven children, three by her current partner, Wilson. As a child, Sandra was looked after by the local authority after her mother died when she was very young and she was left in the care of her father who was an alcoholic with a history of violence. While Sandra was in a foster placement arranged by the local authority, she made allegations of sexual abuse against her foster father. There was no criminal trial at the time, although it was felt by the professionals working with Sandra at the time it was likely that the allegations were a true account of what had happened to her. She was moved to a different foster placement although this quickly broke down and the history of the rest of Sandra's childhood in care is one of regular placement breakdown and increasing distrust of the adults charged with her care arrangements. As a young adult, Sandra started to misuse alcohol and crack cocaine and developed a personality that was prone to violent or aggressive outbursts whenever she was in a situation in which she did not feel entirely comfortable.

Wilson has two other children with previous partners, both of whom were eventually taken into local authority care. Wilson has mild learning difficulties and a long history of domestic violence and alcohol misuse, although he does not accept that either are problems and therefore does not accept the need for any treatment programme.

The local authority has been involved in three previous sets of care proceedings with this family regarding the four oldest of the seven children, and each of these children are now either in adoptive families or in long-term foster care families.

The children with whom the unit worked were the youngest three: Kara aged five, Leanne aged four and Samuel aged 18 months. The case was allocated to the unit after the children were removed from their parents' care after a serious assault on Sandra by Wilson, whereby he punched her in the face during a heated argument. The incident took place in front of the children and Sandra quickly left to seek medical attention, leaving the children in Wilson's care.

By the time the case was allocated to the unit, the children were placed in two separate foster care placements. This was a planned decision made in order to meet the specific needs of the children, two of whom had need for frequent medical attention. Placing them separately with a high level of sibling contact meant that one foster carer did not become overwhelmed and the placements were more stable and secure.

As is often the case when the local authority is involved with a family where one or both of the parents are extremely aggressive and threatening, there had been a high number of changes in allocated social worker. Previous social workers had faced threats of violence including burns and stabbing, and were regularly verbally abused and spat at. Social workers were advised not to visit alone, which meant that they had to rely on the good will and availability of colleagues in order to complete any visits or contact with the parents.

The challenge for the unit was to work with an aggressive family through the duration of the care proceedings and beyond.

When allocated the case, we initially discussed it at the unit meeting. There was a wealth of information about the family which was helpful and allowed us to look at the previous involvements and to develop a strategy for our own involvement. It was apparent that one of the disruptive interactions the parents used was to seek a very high level of contact with the social workers that was time consuming. It could be up to ten phone calls and two or three visits to the office each day.

It was decided that the unit coordinator, being the first contact for all service users, was initially to try to deal with the situation on the telephone when the parents made contact. If this failed, she would make an appointment for them to see the social worker or consultant social worker. At this point any further contact would be only to ensure there was no emergency and to reiterate the appointment.

Using the skills of the unit coordinator this way, the social workers were able to avoid becoming involved in the time-consuming daily arguments with the parents. The unit was also able to plan for each appointment and how to keep themselves safe when the parents were present.

The unit coordinator's role developed significantly over the duration of the case. As the parents were unable to build the negative relationships with the social workers that they were usually able to do, they began to build a positive relationship with the unit coordinator. They began to see her as a more neutral person who was able to assist them when they were feeling anxious about the children while they were not in their care.

The unit coordinator was able to keep them up to date with all aspects of the children's placements, and gradually the parents began to develop trust in the local authority and as their anxiety decreased, so did the level of their contacts.

The weekly unit meeting was essential for ensuring that all unit members were clear about the plans for the children and any appointments for the coming week, so the unit coordinator could field the calls appropriately. It enabled the unit to make a plan for the week's interventions and to reflect on the previous week and to see what had worked and what had not.

The role of the children's practitioner within this case was to develop a relationship with the children in their foster placements and with the two sets of foster carers. As the children's practitioner role is not involved in the court process, it was decided that, in this case, they were best placed to be a consistent presence for the children and support for the foster carers. The visits could be planned and regular, with the consultant social worker supervising at each unit meeting and accompanying or asking the social worker to accompany where observation for the court may make it necessary.

For the consultant social worker, having the children's practitioner available to build a close relationship with the children meant that the unit was able to undertake much more comprehensive work with the family. Contacts were observed regularly and work done with the children regarding their experiences at home and their wishes and feelings for the future. The relationships they were able to build with their foster families were observed, and all of this information was fed back to the unit through the unit meeting. The children's practitioner kept a clear record of each visit or observation and this could then be used by the consultant social worker in their assessments and when writing reports for the court.

Minutes of each unit meeting were taken by the unit coordinator and records of the discussion regarding each individual child and family were in turn placed on the case files.

The skills of the unit clinician were used in an indirect manner in this particular case. The children were young and were not displaying any behaviour that was of concern to their respective foster families, nor were they finding the regular contact sessions distressing in any way. Therefore, introducing them to an additional professional seemed somewhat unnecessary, and the parents were clear that they would not engage with any therapeutic work themselves. However, in order to process the information from the children's practitioner and social workers as well as continually evaluate our strategies for managing the parents, the unit meeting became, to a certain degree, a therapeutic supervision led by the clinician. The clinician proposed conversations and questions that were designed to manage the parents' aggressive behaviour while still engaging in meaningful work with them about understanding their relationship and continuing to assess their ability to change or adapt and meet the children's needs.

The clinician and the children's practitioner worked closely together with the clinician offering almost clinical supervision to the children's practitioner in order to maximise the effectiveness of her visits to the children and also in working with the foster carers who had developed strong and positive relationships with the children.

The consultant social worker and the social worker both continued to work with the parents regarding the court work and long-term planning for the children. This included a family group conference with extended family members on both sides of the family. Some family members had been assessed previously but others had come forward once they had been told about the care proceedings by the parents.

The family group conference was planned carefully during a unit meeting that was attended by the family group conference coordinator and the unit as a whole. We were able to use our knowledge of the family and the skills of the clinician to formulate questions for the family members to consider when discussing the children. It enabled the needs of the children to remain at the centre of every discussion that was held rather than the needs of the parents, which can sometimes happen, however skilled the family group conference coordinator may be.

The outcome was an agreement with the family, including the parents, that while they hoped the children could return to their care, unless there were significant changes it was an unlikely outcome. Therefore, alternative arrangements had to be made.

Two family members on the paternal side came forward to be assessed as to whether they were suitable carers and were willing to provide long-term care for the children in the event that they could not return home.

Plans were made for the assessments and the visits were made by either the consultant social worker or the social worker but whoever undertook a visit, the clinician accompanied them. This provided further insight for the assessment but also stimulated a more in-depth discussion with the prospective carers as to what challenges they might face and what tools they might be able to use with help and advice from the clinician in order to meet the children's needs. It was clear from the outset that if successful, both family members would need a reasonable level of support in order to assimilate the children into their families and routines and in order for this to happen, with as little trauma as possible, it was extremely important to develop a clear picture of the strengths and weaknesses within the two families being assessed.

The assessments proved positive and the families were willing to accept a high level of support from the social work unit regarding the introductions to the children as their future carers and the slowly increasing levels of contact between the children and their extended family members. These introductions and contact arrangements were planned with family members for dates and times that would be convenient, but the unit coordinator had the primary role in the logistics of ensuring that transport providers, contact centres, family members and foster carers were all clear about who was meant to be where and when.

The children's practitioner was the primary link with the children in respect of their contact arrangements and accompanied them on their first few sessions until they were clearly comfortable enough with the sessions. The children's practitioner would then catch up with the children afterwards and ask them how the contact was, whether they were comfortable and what their wishes and feelings were at each stage.

The social worker and consultant social worker were the primary link with the professionals and the court at this stage. The weekly unit meeting was a helpful time for ensuring that all information was shared, but in this case, it was discussed almost every day at this very busy and important stage, often more than once as there was so much happening and so much information coming into the unit.

The parents were determined that they were not going to separate from one another but sadly, their violent behaviour at home remained entrenched and the assessment of the social work unit was that the children would not be safe if they returned to their parents' care. It was also apparent that neither parent was able to change enough to enable them to care for the children appropriately. The care plans were agreed in court and once the social work unit had completed some practical assistance tasks, such as purchasing beds, the children were placed in two groups, one of two and the youngest on their own. The split was decided on in consultation with the birth parents and the extended family as part of a second family group conference that also discussed levels of contact for the future as well as which family members would assist the parents if they were struggling with the arrangements and were upset or confused. This was intended to give them someone to talk with whom they knew and respected, and it was hoped that this would prevent the placements from being exposed to behaviours that may have put them under pressure and led to a possible breakdown.

The placements were made successfully following a well-supported series of introductory visits that were gradually extended to include overnights, weekends and finally a whole week. Both placements were visited at a minimum of every other day during these stays in order to offer both the children and carers the support they needed as well as to enable the social work unit to give the parents up-to-date information each day without them (the parents) having to approach the placements directly themselves and potentially start unsettling the children so early in their stay.

Over the following weeks and months it became apparent that the placements were becoming increasingly robust and the children were developing successful attachments to their new carers while the parents managed to maintain a level of contact that worked for the children without placing too much pressure on any one individual.

I will leave the story of this family at this stage and consider how the advantages of the Reclaiming Social Work model enabled the consultant social worker to be supported by the rest of the unit to keep Kara, Leanne and Samuel within their own extended family and out of the care of the local authority.

This case involved a family that was a high level consumer of social work, although in the traditional 'team' model, where social workers are one of a number of social workers within a team, the time was spent reacting to the parents' problems and difficult behaviour. In the Reclaiming Social Work model the unit is allowed to develop strategies to manage the parents' behaviour that in turn creates more time for the unit to assess the children's needs, to assess the family's strengths and to create a plan to meet the long-term needs of all three children.

The consultant social worker now had the freedom and resources to look beyond the initial problem and to persist in attempting to identify family members who could look after Kara, Leanne and Samuel where previously it is possible that they would have remained in foster care once the crisis had passed, and it was clear that the children could not return to their parents. The extended family members needed an extremely high level of practical and emotional support in order to care for the children, and the visits and advice from the unit clinician were valuable in helping the carers understand the children's behaviour and how they, as carers, could help the children to understand what was happening and subsequently settle them into their placements with as little trauma as possible.

The weekly unit meeting was essential in analysing the amount of information that the unit was able to collate over a relatively short period of time. It was in this meeting that the pace the unit was able to work at became apparent. In the traditional model it would have taken one social worker an enormous amount of work hours to gather, analyse and assess the information, offer the support to three different groups within the same family, as well as manage a caseload of children all with competing needs and priorities. However, the unit was able to manage this level of work by dividing tasks and sharing responsibility for the well-being of the children as well as maintaining a forward momentum.

The positive outcome in this case of ensuring that Kara, Leanne and Samuel were all sustained within their birth family was completed in good time, and the unit working as a whole under the management and guidance of the consultant social worker was the reason there was no delay.

Most people who enter the social work profession do so in order to make sure that children are looked after safely in their own family whenever possible; however, they are not always working in a system that enables them to do their job to the best of their ability. Working with even the most challenging families in the Reclaiming Social Work model allows experienced social workers to work at a faster pace, to complete more comprehensive assessments and to find more imaginative solutions to family problems.

Commentary by Professor Stephen Scott

This chapter is very helpful, as it spells out in considerable detail the process by which the family work was undertaken. The author is honest about the feelings and values social work engenders, including the desire to enable children to remain in their families wherever possible. Some readers might think that the 'right' answer was obtained here, since the children remained in the wider family, and hence out of long-term public care, but were given the chance to grow up in a loving environment where secure attachments were possible without the fear of witnessing violent attacks. What is striking is the benefit for the team of being given the space and encouragement to *think* about the process of what was going on with this family. This enabled them to identify the coercive interactions that for the family had become habitual. 'Naming the game' here was followed by a thoughtful response, so that while the team did answer calls, they did so in such a way that the family got no gain from being aggressively controlling, and as predicted by social learning theory (SLT), they subsequently stopped behaving this way and began to enjoy less strife-ridden interchanges with the social services department. I suspect that this thoughtful and effective piece of work would not have been possible without the support of the team in which a senior consultant was able to provide experienced case (or 'clinical', in the Reclaiming Social Work model) leadership, and not just tick boxes. This was social work at its best. I am not sure the parents in the family were, as the chapter title hints, able to move beyond their own histories, insofar as their children were moved from their care, just as they themselves were removed from their parents. However, the next generation will have a far better chance to get out of the cycle, and we should remember Rutter and Quinton's (1984) study that showed that even when raised in residential homes, not all the girls grew up to be inadequate as mothers. In that study, despite their very difficult start in life, half were able to go on to be 'good enough' mothers, a tribute to the potential resilience and power for recovery within all human beings.

References

Rutter, M. and Quinton, D. (1984) 'Long-term follow-up of women institutionalized in childhood: Factors promoting good functioning in adult life.' *British Journal of Developmental Psychology 2*, 3, 191–204.

CHAPTER 11

Seen and Heard

The Unfolding Story of Reclaiming Social Work Through the Eyes of a Children's Practitioner

Charlie Clayton

I joined Hackney's Children and Young People's Service (CYPS) in January 2008. The preliminary research and development had been undertaken and Reclaiming Social Work was being implemented in social work with children and families for the first time. My story concerns how it produced what Gregory Bateson describes as 'the difference which makes a difference' (Bateson 2000, p.99) in the organisation's work, and in my own practice. Bateson's phrase has many implications for social services' provision to citizens and their communities. The review of methodology in Chapter 2 has explored these implications and weaved in the many other strands that comprise the way the project has developed to date.

But first, it seems helpful to set out what, for me, Reclaiming Social Work seems to have achieved since its inception as social work practice in January 2008:

- the development of a methodology that is amenable to analysis and review, that is flexible and adaptive, and which responds coherently to those needs that are expressed by the social culture of which the service is a part

- the acquisition, maintenance and articulation of practitioner skills that are relevant to the demands made on the service, and on its context

- the secure prioritisation of vulnerable children's safety and well-being

- a formalisation of the CYPS's intentions in its work with its principal service users

- a re-think on its relationship with the wider community, and other public services

- the reclaiming of a sense of direction, of confidence, of expertise and of gravitas in the way we go about our work.

Early days

My first day found me pitched into Hackney's old offices in Morning Lane, a grim grey elbow of road leading to the A12 between a mixture of dilapidated terraces and grey estates that looked bred for violence. Dotted around the desks, people stared and tapped away in the cold glow of their monitors. Someone would fly in through the door past the gate-keeping administrator, to talk volubly and with evident distress about something they'd just seen or done, before settling down in front of a screen of their own to type furiously, in what looked like a carefully modulated panic attack. Outside the largest of the main rooms, middle managers sat in long, high-ceilinged cubicles devoid of decoration and painted a nasty shade of green. Sometimes one of the social workers would leap up from their desk or, if a little more in hand, step purposefully towards the cubicles for a consultation. When they had no one to see, the team managers pecked at their keyboards in a quite different manner from their subordinates, reminding me of sad caged birds that can't see the sky.

I came to work in Hackney after a previous career in an entirely different field. Dissatisfied and somewhat alienated by the developments in media that accompanied the expansion of the industry into 'digital', I undertook a PGCE (Postgraduate Certificate of Education) at the Institute of Education but found its priorities differed from my own. I nevertheless observed that I seemed capable of achieving worthwhile outcomes for children with problems in schools. So, while working for very little money, with pupils who evidently found it impossible to get along without close supervision, I started further training at Birkbeck in child-oriented psycho-dynamic counselling. I did a little work for Kids Company on the side. I joined a private enterprise providing 'packages' to children excluded from mainstream education, first as a teacher and then as an education case manager. When Hackney's CYPS posted vacancies for children's practitioners, I applied – albeit with substantial scepticism.

I held assumptions all too common, particularly among those involved (as I had been) in providing the population with its news. Social work? Dreadful! Hopeless! Poorly skilled and managed, equivocal at best in terms of its achievements, and populated from one end to the other by busybody do-gooders with a vested interest in telling other people how to live their lives. Social workers took children. They brewed up fantastic stories about witch covens to justify their outrageous incursions into other people's liberties. They made everyone feel bad about even standing next to a child. On the other hand, the role – a new one to social work practice – seemed to offer a better position from which to engage in the kind of work I wanted to do.

The interview process seemed absurdly challenging. After answering an unseen three-part 45-minute essay question that began, 'What do you understand by the phrase "good enough parenting"?', and undertaking two tortuous verbal reasoning tests, I retired to a local pub feeling full of doom. I called my wife and said, 'I can't believe it. I think I've just blown getting a job with the council.' Now, I can see why such a failure wouldn't be shameful in any way at all. Standards are high at Hackney's CYPS. Very high. Yes, there's some accommodation for different skills profiles. Yes, it's certainly recognised that pressures of the work can force errors. But from the beginning, there was something in the air that recalled the intensity, the creativity and the necessary precision which organises live television production. The thing felt a little like a television channel launch. People talked fast, questioned one another about what they were doing, batted ideas back and forth. And it was all about the outcome. Government procedures were being followed, but the rest seemed, well, loose. It was clear that I'd need to get inventive, and quickly, just to stand still in the place. And standing still was certainly not being encouraged.

The induction week offered more troubling cases, as case studies, behavioural-based interventions and systemic approaches to practice were advanced as benchmarks of effective, legitimate social work practice. I remember thinking that the newly conceived consultant social worker role looked like a whole bag of trouble. Like an underlying backbeat, the whole thing seemed to be organised around something called 'evidence base'. Now knowing what that means, I have a problem with this in the context of social science. One of the journeys I've undertaken – alongside Isabelle and the organisation she and Steve described conceiving in Chapter 1 – from child counsellor to student social worker, from carer to enabler, from concerned individual to outright activist, has been to understand that it's the arguments around the meaning of what's happening which comprise where the real meat of children's social work keeps its juice. For example, a social work practitioner observes an alcoholic mother unable to care for her children, a school sees wasted opportunities for their pupils' young minds, the parent says she's just coping with stress. Each of these perspectives needs to be considered in formulating a course of action if all of the parties are to remain engaged and committed to reaching a more satisfactory conclusion. Facts, when you find them in children's social care, can prove slippery.

During one afternoon we looked at a sample case in depth. Real or fabricated? I'm not sure. Certainly the short film we watched was created with a camera and actors. Medical students make a similar use of cadavers. A family was living in chaotic, filthy accommodation. Drug purchasers in and out of the place, feeding in the money that kept things going, and perhaps messing about unhealthily with the children during their visit. Children all over the place: climbing across the counters, destroying the walls and furniture, filling nappies if they had them and leaving deposits if they didn't. Some unwholesome mutual self-comforting behaviour. Heaps of rubbish and a smashed car outside were being used as climbing frames. There were indications that the parents were trying to provide some form of care, but the situation was a disaster. Social workers were worried about safety on home visits. Responses of the 'responsible adults' were evidently randomised by misery, by fear, by ignorance about the options, by shame and by a diet that emphasised drink and drug intake rather than more conventional forms of nourishment.

Sitting at a table with Audrey and me (it had now been decided I'd work in her unit) were Esther, a social work clinician[1] with a Master's in Family Therapy; Bola, an administrator evidently packed with powerful but gently delivered energy; and the personnel of another unit. We started to thrash the thing out. Our social worker, Peggy, was abroad and would be familiarised with unit working alongside another cohort the following week. Our first task was to assess a number of statements about the family, providing reasons for our view that they were either fact or opinion. I was surprised to find this rather more difficult than I'd

---

1   A term describing any person with healthcare responsibilities who sees people presenting with health issues, within the context of a larger organisation, possessing a professionally accredited qualification and subject to certified guidelines in respect of their practice.

imagined. I discovered I was packed full of preconceptions. I realised I didn't really have any faith in the family's capacities to sort things out. At all. Remove the children! An idea that immediately ran into a brick wall: this was far from being an unusual story. Plenty of poor people put up with worse. At least the kids didn't seem to be actively set on deliberate destruction of one another or their parents. At least there was no evidence of prostitution, or of adults engaged in destructive sexual activity. As far as it was possible to tell, no one appeared to have become psychotic. Or not yet, anyway.

With an assurance that I suddenly found rather shocking, Audrey stepped in to moderate the responses of the people around the table. I'd been used to the assertive, often black and white thinking that drives plenty of television production. Here, it was clear that rhetoric really wasn't going to cut it. The temptation was to make assumptions, draw back and start directing action to quell the problem. But one of social work's difficulties is that you're dealing with real people who have every right and need of their own autonomy. You can't think for them. You can't confine their behaviours to make them safe, or not for long. And if you go to law for that purpose, you produce other problems, and plenty of costs. So ideally, you need to generate a process that's going to result in different perspectives in families, ones that generate different behaviours. Anxiety needs to be moderated or mediated so that some new thinking can happen. Having sifted through the difference between what really were the hard facts and what were feelings disguised as assertions to achieve a sense of certainty amidst all the confusion and trouble, we began to elaborate a plan.

Limitations of space here, and perhaps of the time you can devote to reading, prevents describing that plan. In any case it's just one of between 60 and 90 cases any Access/Duty and Assessment team will be carrying at one time. Find out the facts, limit the factors and impacts posing immediate risks, refer to community services or – if the situation looks likely to remain severe for a while, to the longer-term department in which I work now. I was struck by the mixture of clarity and solicitation the people around me brought to the discussion. Esther took what family therapists call a 'meta-position' that began with the broadest picture of the situation, and refined it down to the relationships between family members, the beliefs and ideas they seemed to hold in respect of how they should live their lives, the way adult care seemed to operate in respect of the children's needs, right down to particular details observed during the social work visit itself (or, more accurately, the camera's account of the roles played by the short film's performers). Clearly there was significant risk of harm to children here. The question was: 'What are we going to do about it?'

Astonished by the whole experience of the week, I went home and applied to study systems oriented therapy at the Institute of Family Therapy (IFT). The shortest of possible conversations with Debra Philip and clinical manager, Amanda Kardouche, seem to have been the source of this decision. They encouraged me to consider that counselling work in schools could only take the consequences of deficits in care so far. When children go home, their situation is no different. When one of them is managing, there's no guarantee a sibling isn't going to walk into the counselling room to take their place. In fact, chances are that if you can motivate some resilience in one child, then the abuse is likely to be transferred elsewhere within the family 'system'.

Something I find frustrating in conversations with people who work outside the field is their difficulties in recognising that, for perpetrators, the abuse of children serves a purpose. It's extremely rare for people to harm children without thinking about it. Such people are dangerous and belong in Broadmoor. Many of them end up there. But that's a very small sector of the population, far smaller than the number of families struggling with severe poverty, with limited understanding about how to get out of it and with all the colours of feeling that make them believe they're simply too 'different' to imagine that their own lives, and their actions in respect of others, are going to achieve anything other than unhappiness and harm. Sometimes their children suffer as a result. Social 'work' isn't about imposing conformity. But where there's clear and well researched evidence to indicate that, for example, a child coming to school with an empty stomach and the sounds of their parents beating and being beaten inside the dubious cosiness of an alcoholic or other haze still ringing in their ears, it seems reasonable to act on the hypothesis that they're likely to get less out of their classes than children from more stable homes.

The hospital team: pre-birth assessments of parenting

My early days with the hospital team were characterised by, among other things, evident conflict between Audrey's practice priorities and Esther's. Our offices were cramped, leaving me separated from my unit in another room. Here, I was kindly mentored in the basics by a helpful social worker called Ali. Meena, group manager for the hospital units, had a cubicle more remote than the ones down at Morning Lane. She was always welcoming, and I was delighted to find that despite my comparative ignorance about the business we were engaged in, she was more than happy to offer advice and provide additional direction in my work and my learning. But I sensed an increasing discomfort in the way she asserted and defined the boundaries around our assessments and preliminary work with the families of 'unborns'. Looking back, I find it hard to recollect why the therapeutic and social work perspectives were in such manifest conflict. Perhaps the two years' training I undertook at IFT before beginning my current Master's course in Social Work helped me to put them together in my mind. In any case, the struggle of Reclaiming Social Work's early days lost us some talented people.

Nevertheless, the energy and developing synergies between social work roles and external agencies felt palpable. Hospital consultant social workers were attending weekly medical forums – SCBU ('special care' baby unit), perinatal mental health (planning and reviewing new and expectant mothers' care plans), SAU (specialist addiction unit) – and actively promoting considerations of health and well-being associated with families' care of children. These comprised an ongoing consideration of the link between hospital care and 'care in the community'. So this is what 'useless' social workers do, I thought.

Social work with families referred because of concerns about their capacity to manage after a birth are inevitably speculative. The implications of the event itself, under the scrutiny of a government department with access to the courts, further distorts information sharing between families and social services. In consequence, the hospital department's principal focus is on the arrangement of community resources that will safeguard the baby and its care when it goes home. A case will be held for a few weeks following the delivery, to see how things develop. If problems continue to surface, the family will be referred on to the long-term team.

Alberta, a children's practitioner in 'Rapid Response' – a quick-fire service with a remit to resolve acute crises in families and prevent their children being removed to foster care – one day suggested that I come and take a look at how the role worked there. I need to warn you that the day provided me with a whole new view on what the Reclaiming Social Work documentation describes as 'The way we do things here'. Please accept my apologies if you find my description of the day exhausting. There was a lot to take in.

Her unit's work initially seemed pretty much as I'd expected. From 9 o'clock there was a quiet hum of activity: recording and sharing information about ongoing interventions, reviewing the efficacy of current strategies, making calls to service users and other agencies, synchronising diaries for joint visits to families and so on. Alberta sketched out her involvement with an adolescent girl where deficits in her care were making the necessity of fostering a possibility. She invited me to come to meet her later in the day. As something of an emergency service, Rapid Response runs along lines similar to those of an ambulance crew: periods of preparation and follow-up interspersed with bursts of intense activity.

Group manager Mark Stancer popped in for a quick chat with the consultant social worker. A family already referred to the long-term Children in Need (CIN) service had suddenly taken a severe turn for the worse. The situation was complicated. Justifications for extreme and detrimental behaviours were being made by different parties. There was a general mix of expressed anger, pleas for assistance and children being forced into situations where there could be no reasonable expectation that they'd thrive. A principal focus among the family was the uselessness of the work being done by the CIN service. As a result, and in preference to making an application for a removal order, Mark's department had been contacted for assistance.

Five minutes' conversation with the consultant social worker, the social worker and Alberta (clinical posts are '0.5', as they are shared between two units – the clinician was with their other unit that day) outlined a 'shaped' intervention that matched each practitioner to a particular role in addressing the case's concerning issues. The idea was to diminish the heightened feelings – 'affect' for psychotherapists, the impact of cortisol (a hormone produced by the body in response to stress) for psychologists with a more biological bent. This was to be achieved by going to the home and reviewing, through coordinated conversations and determinations of action, the thinking and behaviours that were placing the children at a substantially increased risk of harm. Sophisticated stuff! My presence, with no particular part to play, would have watered down or perhaps even derailed the intervention. Mark therefore suggested I might want to have a chat with two other managers, in two small offices along yet another corridor, while the unit set off.

Tina McElligot managed Hackney's Preventative Services, first under Debra, then later as its head of service when Debra's health began to deteriorate. A network of community-based resources that address specific social problems experienced by families – parenting support, substance misuse and prevention services, the Family Intervention Service's intensive, whole family service at home which intends to reduce youth violence and offending behaviour, etc. – Preventative Services offer interventions without a statutory component. Families can self-refer, or otherwise gain access through the Joint Access Review Panel (JARP).[2] Tina provided me with a whirlwind tour of its workings. I was again struck by the design and implementation's intense concentration of will, effort and attention to detail.

Ten minutes later, my head full of aspirations along with fears about my ability to meet the organisation's requirements, I left Tina's office and opened the door to Eric DeMello's. Somewhat typically of my experience within the Reclaiming Social Work model, he immediately presented me with a solution that depended on my own motivation to make the corollary commitment. His pragmatism set out the critical importance for families of well managed transitions out of the intense environment of CYPS, into the plethora of resources Tina had just outlined. He talked about citizens' rights, and the moderation of state control. We also talked about motorbikes, and his favoured haunts for the excellent, cheap ethnic food scattered all over the borough. I left feeling human again. It was a day that took many weeks to digest. Fortunately, Alberta's meeting with the teenage girl took place in a local cafe, where we all found something that helped the medicine go down.

Along with the intensive, self-critical, reflective high energy work, I was happy to find some room for a bit of similarly intensive play. Two consultant social workers in Rapid Response – Risthardh and Stephen – assisted me in addressing these deficits by hauling me out for drinks after work and introducing me to an absurd number of highly gifted practitioners working across the service. They taught me not to be ashamed about shouting ever louder in political and practice debates

---

2   A multi-agency review panel, JARP assesses the merit of referrals from social work units for families with complex needs that may be met by non-statutory agencies. Assessment and evaluation are similar to the processes by which units themselves plan casework. Other panels handling other configurations of complexity – concerning high level risk, interagency collaboration, more substantial resource allocation, plans associated with foster care and so on – are regularly convened and reflect the broader systems-based approach increasingly characteristic in public service agencies.

while more indifferent pub customers watched football and played pool. Above all else, they convinced me about the intrinsically social nature of the work we were doing, firmly situating it within the context of 'everyday people', and of the highly functional working relationships that together aggregate as the overarching paradigm of the Reclaiming Social Work project.

Random conversations also developed in alarmingly rapid fashion, evidently touching fire to wider and wider groups of interested, motivated and enthusiastic people. I found that co-workers were keen to share contacts within their particular expertise, to form connections that would move the whole organisation forward. Sophie, for example, was engaged in a project collating data on community services. Her overview of connections between CYPS and partnership agencies formed the kernel of a venture in which Eric encouraged me to explore possibilities concerning more effective care planning and information sharing in this area.

Some things can grow too quickly! The ground work laid by Isabelle, Steve, Debra, Clare and Mary seemed to have effectively turned the whole borough into ground fertile for the growth of 'change'. My previous experience in communications and production management for broadcasters dovetailed very neatly into the collaborative, strengths-based, solution-focused values espoused by the CYPS as a whole. What I lacked, and didn't realise I lacked, was the insight into potential problems associated with a disregard for the politics. The senior management's substantial understanding, not to mention delicacy in pursuing their aims (I don't altogether buy into Isabelle's gung ho presentation of Reclaiming Social Work's developments in Chapter 12 – she has a quick, neat and tidy mind that swiftly sets aside what's unhelpful, I think) were missing from my plans. Unsurprisingly, and shortly in advance of a meeting to which a number of senior figures from various agencies, including Hackney's central information services department, had accepted invitations, I became aware of rumblings. It seemed expedient to send out a speedy flock of cancellations and grimly await my fate. Except that it didn't come. I was aware of my mistake, spent time understanding the whys and wherefores of it, and took care not to repeat it. To the best of my knowledge, there were no repercussions.

Meanwhile, progress seemed to be proceeding in resolving the twin remits of unit working as set out in the Reclaiming Social Work model – on the one hand, child protection; on the other, enabling families to recognise and respond productively in addressing deficits in their childcare. Above all, the 'voice of the child' was not being lost. Nevertheless, a year in, we felt the 'dip' on the front line too. It prompted our unit to reconsider whether we were happy with what we were doing. In the odd way that the work environment seems to shape communications and the focus of social work, we began to think that we weren't working too well. Esther decided she'd be better off in a more medical environment, and left to join a Child and Adolescent Mental Health Service (CAMHS). Difficulties among Peggy's family abroad took her out of the country for a further extended period. Audrey, Bola and I were glum.

I also had an eye on the systems oriented therapy training due to start in September. Hackney was now commissioning IFT to provide the programme in-house. During my first year, I had attended courses that equipped me with the more traditional tools of social work with children and families: child protection issues, procedures and practice; the legal framework; clinical interventions such as life-story book work and so on. I was looking forward to acquiring the skills to work more closely with families from a relational perspective, but concerned that work within the hospital team, with its remit of short-term assessment, would not provide me with adequate opportunities as a student to develop my practice. Audrey had itchy feet too. With our unit substantially disassembled, Audrey and I moved together to the long-term CIN service.

Gathering pace with Children in Need: long-term work with families

If Access/Duty and Assessment departments try to work out what's going on in families referred to children's social services, CIN departments take on more extended interventions where crisis management and community-based services haven't resolved the presenting issues. Audrey's prodigious appetite for work met with our new clinician's encyclopaedic grasp of theory and deeply grounded approach to the psychology of family dynamics. Jeremy's response on learning that I intended to train in systemic practice was to promote that learning curve from the beginning. A few days after we'd been assigned some office space, he handed me a small raft of papers and articles that he imagined would provide me with a good start. The contents of those papers still resonate with me today.

Jeremy's approach to community-based therapy with 'service users' (rather than clients working with him by choice) seemed essentially uncomplicated, straightforward and practical. I was subsequently to discover that this was achieved through prodigious prior reflection, reading and case discussion. In retrospect, it's hard to identify what I picked up in preparing for the course and what became more evident later, but one way or another the therapeutic intention of Hackney's CYPS became clear to me for the first time: we're not trying to solve families' problems; we're there to help them find different ways of functioning so that the problems go away. A family is a 'system' of interrelated relationships, communications, beliefs, 'scripts' (that is, linked causal chains of behaviour and meaning that begin with people's expectations of one another) and a complex mix of individual and shared identities. The system also incorporates others involved with the family. Friends and associates, partners of one kind or another, teachers, health workers, legal advisers, police and probation workers, therapists, specialists in domestic violence, agencies promoting specific cultural and ethnic agendas... they're all part of the 'system' too.

Within the family's system there are resources that may address and resolve the issues identified as problematic in the referral, during preliminary assessments and during the course of the intervention. For the purposes of face-to-face social work, systems oriented interventions represent perhaps the most surefooted route to a fundamental principle and validation of social work's legitimacy, bearing similarities with medicine's Hippocratic Oath: anti-oppressive practice (AOP). Among other things, systemic perspectives recognise that fists, tears, sex working and substance misuse are ways of making statements about what's happening too. As, of course, are neglect, violence and other abuses of children. The systemic paradigm incorporates other mainstays of social work practice: 'task-centred', 'solution-focused' and so on.

Another major acquisition at the unit's 'inception' was a social worker called Emma. Emma brought a stack of experience from North American 'children's homes' and a further stint for a UK youth offending team (YOT). Her thinking was very clear and specific. Whatever the circumstances, it was hard to spot a moment when she wasn't fully 'switched on' and ready for action. Stress was only evident in the way she'd walk very slowly between the office desks, arms swung loosely by her sides, a far-off gaze in her eye.

Partnering the systems oriented perspective, Reclaiming Social Work incorporates social learning theory (SLT), a theory that outlines the processes and issues associated with learning by observation, through imitation and from behaviours that are 'modelled' by others. It highlights the difference between behavioural and social change – something very much at the heart of systems oriented work – and learning. Or to put it more bluntly, it recognises the importance of wisdom, of personal knowledge and of the functional benefits associated with autonomy. In practical terms, this represents another aspect of AOP: protecting service users' rights and interests, promoting their independence and personal agency within the context of their circumstances and acknowledging their rights. It comprises a crucial tool in the Reclaiming Social Work model's application in Hackney, where we are involved with families approaching our concerns from a very diverse range of cultural beliefs, values and languages. It allows us to find common ground concerning the frequently contentious issue, 'What exactly is it that the CYPS wants to happen here?' Negotiation around the issues this raises, not only with families and communities but also during the course of interagency partnerships, in research and in conversations with the media, forms another core aspect of the Reclaiming Social Work model. I should add that Emma very generously waived her place on the course with IFT so that I could take it, instead joining the SLT programme before beginning the systemic training the following year.

Finding a compatible unit coordinator initially proved tricky. Our first came from a very different work background. She decided she didn't like the position within a few weeks, and left. Nadine – insouciant, hard-headed and a Hackney resident all her life, fit the bill much better. Previous work for a fashion house had evidently given her a taste for dealing with self-pressurising people. She brought a real-life perspective that complemented the different styles of working and thinking shared between Audrey, Jeremy, Emma and myself. For the first time, I felt that our unit was fully formed.

A children's practitioner in context

As a children's practitioner, the immediate benefits of the resources offered by these colleagues was obvious. For a children's practitioner, the main priority is to ensure that the 'voice of the child' remains present in any arrangements concerning their care. I imagine that all social workers begin with a resolute commitment to working with, safeguarding and responding to that voice. The difficulties in persisting with this commitment are, however, enormous. Children referred to social services have, by and large, fallen substantially outside the moderating influences of education, law and/or health. Of course these don't by any means represent the totality of the social 'world' in which they live and grow. Good social work certainly isn't about enforcing compliance with the state. Its institutions provide, however, the checks and balances to individual discovery that, roughly speaking, offer the kinds of tramlines that will make it easier for children to manage in the world as they proceed towards adulthood. The same story of disconnection and conflict between individuals and state agencies is often reflected in the personal life histories of their parents and families too. Such families rarely regard their first contact with CYPS in a positive light.

The picture is further complicated by the differing values accorded to gender roles, money, marriage, leisure activities, food and living customs and all the rest that go to make up contemporary, multi-cultural Britain. And complicated again by the intergenerational stories generated among the children of migrant families living in England (first, second and third generations…). Such families often need to incorporate a substantial change to their circumstances, resources and way of life. Those referred to children's social care have evidently struggled with aspects of this process. Frequently they describe difficulties in assimilation associated with new circumstances that are perhaps alien or even unwelcomed in their culture of origin. Parents can also, quite naturally, see their progenies' assumption of competence and independence in this 'new' world as a compromise, or even a disloyalty to the values that in their own life seem quite 'good enough'.

Together, these factors present a robust barrage of difficulties, for the families, and for those agencies with a particular remit to improve their capacities to manage independently. Education and health encompass core values and benefits that are more universally recognised in intercultural contexts, although of course their methods and guiding principles differ widely across the globe. Law is, of course, the law, but again there is generally global consensus that if people are going to work within a unified structure of social organisation that delineates rights and responsibilities, this begins with recognition of its existence. In this respect, social work is unique in attempting to guide the populace's own power in addressing those issues that the other institutions are evidently unable to regulate. Social work currently relies on research and practices that are not primarily its own. Unlike medicine or law, it does not have a paradigmatic language. We seek to corral consensus and commitment from service users who have experienced substantial failure in their engagements with other public institutions. And by failure, I'm referring to the simple fact that these other institutions haven't been sufficiently effective to secure the family's liberty to live without unusual interference and involvement of state agencies. Such families and citizens are operating from a position of social poverty.

Under these circumstances, a social work practitioner is quite naturally motivated to become risk-averse, to become depressed and dependent, at times clinging to institutional authority in a way that directly contradicts the experience of the people we are trying to help. At other times we can become lost in the thoughts and feelings that constitute the troubled worlds in which we work on a daily basis. For me, the unit brought together under Audrey in CIN seemed to offer a means to persist in this environment. There were the warm, professional and active relational partnerships within the unit itself. There was the assistance of more senior managers when we found things seemed to be getting on top of or away from us. There was the training. There were the bits and pieces of equipment – a developing IT system, mobile phones to keep us in touch and on which to make impromptu notes, a small set of pool cars to transport children and family members in crisis, safely and with competence. There was the extensive work being done by CYPS to forge productive relationships and mutual understanding of the work and priorities, between ourselves and partnership agencies. There was the methodological research being carried out by Hackney in collaboration with the London School of Economics and Political Science (LSE), at IFT, and (for managers) at the Tavistock and Portman clinics. There were the links with government, and the senior management's discourses there that we were not party to, but were nevertheless aware of.

From time to time, you'd hear about a group of consultant social workers who had been talking with Members at the House of Lords. Workers who'd proved their worth and needed a break from direct casework were redeployed to set up new, research-based services such as the multi-systemic treatment foster care (MTFC) team, or to refine our approach to legal proceedings, or to reconfigure the style and substance of our interventions and fact-finding among Hackney's gangs. With all this behind me, I felt motivated to engage with children's lives, to live with them through the difficulties in which I found them and the changes to their circumstances that the unit initiated. I felt enabled to take a role in their developing relationships with the other adults responsible for their welfare. Of course the strain remained there in the work. When that disappears while the problems remain in front of you, it is certain that you're missing something significant.

Between casework and developing friendships with colleagues, I became familiar with other CIN units and other parts of the service. Middle and senior managers were, unusually for a social services organisation, evidently happy and even keen to associate with the hoi polloi (because we're not a rabble at all) in what continued to feel like an essentially exuberant venture. The sometimes almost militaristic structure I discerned was, I realised, there to protect the integrity of what we were doing. When you come across circumstances or activities in families that are beyond your capacity to address with equanimity, a remote and thoughtful figure with substantial experience can be very useful. In more recent times, these casual instances have diminished, and have instead been replaced with a much more open access policy during working hours, partly facilitated by the move to new open plan offices behind Hackney's Town Hall. But at this point in the development of the Reclaiming Social Work 'knowledge', and my own understanding of what social work was about, I made use of the privilege to feel comfortable inside the organisation.

Developing a backbone

Confidence in conversation, however, didn't prevent me from encountering difficulties at times in my unit role. The 'voice of the child' is necessarily a partial one within the context of family relationships and communications. There are many perspectives on the most productive means by which a child can be protected, enabled and afforded opportunities for well-being, growth and individuation. At one end, perhaps, is the principle that young people should be provided with everything that they need to explore the world in which they find themselves; at the other, the necessity for respect, the development of sound judgement, the acknowledgement of authority and a readiness to find accord with the decisions made by a family's adults and 'elders'. Like most aspects of this work, the situation is clearly more complex than that, and several perspectives need to be considered together at the same time. Meanwhile, I had started Hackney's systemic practitioner training. My intention at that time and since joining Hackney had been to train as a clinician then move into National Health Service (NHS) therapeutic services. The IFT course changed the way I looked at the world, seemed to encourage me to make better friends with my manner of thinking, and exponentially improved my social work practice.

One sunny afternoon, in the back garden of the Therapeutic Intervention Service's offices, a tremendous argument emerged around the change in the ethnic mix of Hackney's CYPS by comparison with seven years previously, when the status of the local authority's reputation had been somewhat qualified. If it needs spelling out, Hackney was in serious difficulties at the beginning of the millennium, while its employee base more closely reflected the ethnic demography of the borough's population. Some therefore argued that criticism of the service's performance at that time effectively comprised a racist slur. Arguments were made along the lines of 'the public gets what the public wants, and the public wants what the public gets' variety.[3] Concerns were expressed regarding the increasing presence, under Reclaiming Social Work, of white staff from European backgrounds with graduate and postgraduate qualifications. We agreed that this might reflect the richer resources available to this sector of the population. We considered the processes by which such resources become more available to some populations than others, and the part that 'dominant discourse' plays in this state of affairs. This led us quickly to consider the dominant discourses in our own practice, and whether they might conceivably serve the Hackney population better than other discourses and approaches to the work. At this point we realised that we had really only reached the beginning of the discussion, and that in any case we were straying from our principal remit in developing our skills in therapeutic practice.

During the following autumn and winter, one piece of casework stands out in particular. A child excluded from school had been punched in the face by his father, a man with a history of violence and persistent collapses in mental health. Audrey, Jeremy and I went directly to the home when the incident was reported, by the father himself. We felt relieved that our extensive work to develop a good relationship with the father had paid off, but were initially uncertain about how we were

---

3   Respectful acknowledgements are due here to The Jam's 1979 song 'Going Underground'. For what it's worth, it seems to me that the spirit inculcated by that song is rather more present in Hackney now than it was during social work's 'radical' period. There are a number of critiques on modern historical developments in social work, appealing to different political, ideological and theoretical orientations. If you're interested in the subject, I've found *Value Base of Social Work and Social Care: An Active Learning Handbook* (Barnard, Horner and Wild 2008) helpful.

going to help him manage the situation with his son. We were acutely aware of the risks: he might attack the child again, or us, in response to our arrival. We therefore decided against bringing uniformed police with us, and instead advised them of the incident and our intentions. Seated in a Turkish cafe opposite the address, we discussed our strategies and mustered our courage. We considered potential scenarios, and the roles each of us would take in addressing them. We talked about how we felt, its influence on our thinking, and its potential influence on our behaviour as individuals and as a group. We speculated on the meaning our arrival and presence might have for the child, for the father and for the two of them together. We didn't need to discuss why we were doing what we were intending to do – in these circumstances, it was a simple matter of child protection. But the 'how' took a little time.

When we felt ready, we left the cafe and rang the bell at the flat. The father buzzed us in and we climbed to the top floor, where we found the front door open and entered. The father and his son were sitting in the kitchen. Jeremy and Audrey engaged with the father, reassuring him and asking him to tell us again what had happened during the morning. Meanwhile, I spoke quietly with the child, who was frightened, confused and had a cut on his upper lip. There was then a transition during which the father was brought into my conversation with his son. We were then all able to discuss together what might be the best immediate plan. The father recognised that he was unwell and having difficulty in thinking and controlling his feelings. He said how sorry he was to his son, and to us all. His son cried. We agreed that as a provisional step, it would be a good idea for the child to come with us, and for the father to settle himself down in any way he could. I said that I would contact him later in the day, once we had found a place for his son to stay overnight. We then left with the child.

Two days later, I found myself in a fairly remote corner of Kent at 9 p.m. Both the child and his elder brother had been driven to the home of a foster carer identified by our Access to Resources department. Back in London, the majority of the service were having what I subsequently understood to be a fairly 'large' night at the CYPS Christmas party. I took a taxi, train and tube home, then found that I'd left my house keys at work in the rush of collecting the boys' things together, moving between their two emergency placements, and talking with the unit by phone and face-to-face during the course of the move – during a 'removal' it is important to ensure nothing had been forgotten that might encourage additional panic and distress in the child(ren). It was now about 11 p.m. I knocked on a kind neighbour's door and borrowed a ladder. Inside, exhausted, the ladder pulled up after me so as not to offer an open invitation to strangers, I knew we'd need an account of the move, and some details about how the boys seemed to have settled in. The report proved complex, because it needed to address considerations regarding possible problems in the initial phase of the boys' placement. These would need to be passed on to the foster carer's supervising social worker the next morning. I was in bed by about 2 a.m., tired but satisfied. Next morning, the mortice lock on the front door prevented me from using a set of spare keys, so when I left for a 9 a.m. meeting at a school regarding a different family, I had to use the ladder and the window again. As a coda, it seems worth mentioning that the boys are currently in foster care, and manifestly thriving.

This brief episode in our extensive intervention with the boys, their father and the wider family system seems to exemplify significant features of Reclaiming Social Work quite well. Collaborative working, close monitoring of our 'meaning making' as professionals, a readiness to commit ourselves to working responsively within the firm remit of child safety and well-being, together produced a desirable outcome. Risks were undertaken in the planning, which were carefully calculated. We might, for example, have taken police officers with us in consideration of our own safety, but had decided that this might exacerbate the situation and place the child at an increased risk of harm. Prior to the incident, the father was speaking to us several times a day, providing us with opportunities to undertake continual assessment within the context of help and support. Our case management discussions were very detailed. Varied combinations of front-line workers, services and management input continually reviewed aspects and progress in the ongoing intervention. Jeremy's clinical supervision throughout was assured in focusing our effort on the children's long-term welfare, rather than ministering to the very high levels of professional anxiety that the case generated. Audrey was her usually impassioned, forthright, dedicated and clear-sighted self in her overview and management of our collective activities. I felt free to exploit strong relationships I'd developed with both of the children, their father, their mother and other family members, and to make use of my detailed knowledge about the background to the situation with which we were faced.

Substantial concerns had been expressed by Audrey's managers regarding the unit's decision to allow the children to return to their father's care, some months before. We believed, however, that their idolisation of the father would almost certainly have derailed any subsequent attempts to settle them elsewhere, had they not lived through what was certainly a dicey period in his custody. These developments formed part of a larger context encompassing the whole of their very troubled lives, which had included physical and emotional abuse, neglect, abandonment, bereavement and proximity to drugs and guns. They were able to recognise and resolve problematic aspects of care provided previously by their mother, and by a former foster carer who had remained in contact with the boys after they moved back to live with her. Later, the boys were able to recognise the impact of their life experiences on their relationship with one another, and on the difficulties they encountered at school and among their peers. As a result, they were able to reorder their thoughts and to talk about them with myself, Jeremy, Audrey and with other professionals. They were able to recognise that their father was much less capable as a parent than they had hoped.

Of course, such conversations with children never use this kind of language. One of the abiding delights I find in working as a children's practitioner is the necessity to be present and work in a sophisticated way within often complex situations, and then to be able to express myself in ways that a child could understand. For me, that aspect of the role possesses a kind of beauty.

Another turn of the head

The tipping point Isabelle mentions at the end of Chapter 12 was felt by my unit in terms of better access to increasingly diverse and sure-footed support from other services and professionals. Experts and principal figures from minority ethnic communities, service heads from specialist agencies and specialists from within large government services (for example, perinatal mental health at Homerton Hospital) became frequent visitors. They offered summaries of their work and organisations, and the particular features of their specific agency agendas. *Every Child Matters* might indicate, on a casual read, that every institution working with children is working to the same end, but in practice, that's not the case. Education wants children to learn, health wants them to be free of the impingements associated with illness, the law wants them to keep out of trouble. Children's social care attempts to redress the issues that are associated with poverty – in the children themselves, and in their environment. Children's well-being, when you get down to it, is actually rather complicated!

Audrey left on maternity leave and, after a short period with a consultant social worker called Onder at the controls, Emma was promoted to the role. Her social work post was taken by an American social worker, Latonya. At some point during the following summer, over a pint at a canal-side pub (where we'd adjourned after watching units from CIN and Access and Assessment thrash out some extraneous competitive spirit), Mark presented me with strong arguments for altering the course of my professional development. I had just completed the first year of my training with IFT, had signed up for the second, and was loving it. But I was loving the application of its knowledge within the context of social work practice even more. The persuasion wasn't immediate. A psychologist friend working in the NHS told alarming tales about the hours she worked, the conveyor belt of clients she saw, one after another, the pair of expensive trainers she'd bought to provide her with speedy transit between the two offices in which she worked. Worst of all, she felt punished by a system that rewarded successful engagement with clients by ensuring she hardly had room to breathe between sessions. She complained that other psychologists enjoyed the benefits of 'no shows' that left surprising and delightful gaps in their days. But she wasn't prepared even to consider running the risk of working less effectively – suicide is an endemic possibility in her client group – by slackening her application and commitment. I found her experience salutary, and our conversations about it comprised my personal 'tipping point' in the direction of social work with children and families.

At the beginning of 2010, the CYPS moved to new offices combining the substantial majority of local government services – housing, benefits, adults' services, building control, business rates and so on – under one roof. We left behind the grubby old buildings (my own department was turning its back on an enormous and oddly loveable two-storey portacabin) for a 'one-stop shop' that brought us closer to other aspects of public service provision of particular importance to the majority of families my service sees.

The initial discomfort of finding new ways to work together, in a much noisier open plan environment, gave way to a flourishing of the communicative, professionalised, resource-driven, family and child-centred work at the heart of the Reclaiming Social Work model. Within the service, a choice of expertise was suddenly a short walk away. The issues outlined in Professor Munro's *Interim Child Protection* report (Munro 2011) as positive values – better informed and more capable professional partnerships, increased availability of space and time for critical reflection, access to a wide range of skills including expertise that can be 'borrowed' briefly from other departments – were suddenly manifest in the structure of the workplace, rather than simply in the minds and motivations of those involved.

The move seemed to distil what had begun in 2008 in some interesting ways. 'Back office' expertise was suddenly much more available to front-of-house personnel. This brought with it a need for new kinds of boundaries and practices that ensured all practitioners working in the service were enabled by the change, rather than hindered. As far as I can tell, these boundaries have been established, at least in CIN, on the basis of merit. If it works well for service users, we keep it. If it doesn't, we start looking around for another way.

At the end of 2010, Emma moved on. Not to another social work post, but to travel abroad. Systemic practitioners employ a concept called 'whole systems change'. This might refer to the consequences arising from a change of monarch, or of government. It might comprise the shifts in relationships and behaviours that occur when a new child joins a school and an already established class, or a new baby is born into a family. It might be precipitated by the acquisition of a first washing machine, or an internal lavatory, or the assumption of responsibilities for the care of an elderly relative whose own anxieties were previously generating distress throughout a family. Whole systems change is experienced – felt, thought about, talked about and accommodated – by each member of the system. The people who remain involved remain the same; but as a living, responsive, developing and adaptive group, their characteristics and behaviours develop in response to the circumstances of their day-to-day lives. What changes is the patterning of their interactions, their perception of themselves in relation to others both inside and outside the system, and the way in which they perceive what they do. In some ways we're now doing things in the unit that we weren't trying to do while Emma was at the helm. Perhaps one reason for this is that we've prepared ourselves for the change and are accommodating it. Another would be that Rebecca has opened up new doors and possibilities in the way we all work together – no longer Nadine, but now Emmeline, no longer Emma as the social worker, nor Latonya, nor Beverley, but Michelle – ways that are as satisfying as new flavours when the next master chef starts putting their hand to the griddle.

And setting aside the exigencies of child protection work – or, as seems to be becoming manifest within the Reclaiming Social Work model, the work involved in helping families with children in difficulty to find different ways of living – Reclaiming Social Work seems to be going very well indeed. As a children's practitioner and student social worker, I'm dependent on qualified and suitably accredited staff to carry out my part in the overall effort made by Hackney CYPS to provide children living in poverty with a chance of release from its associated burdens. The enthusiasm, willingness (to teach, to learn, to collaborate in accordance with the best practice and values we can come up with) makes the work much easier, or at least much more rewarding. And certainly, evidently more effective than I'd ever have imagined before moving into this line of work. Beyond comprising an inclusive, multi-faceted practice that's clearly benefiting the families we're involved with, Reclaiming Social Work seems to be redressing that other, rather more awful deficit that's been endemic to social work for many years (while selling a lot of newspapers) – the one that leaves us clueless about how to remake and remodel the circumstances pushing children towards miserable, painful, unproductive or actively pernicious lives, lives that can spread and engender damage among those with whom they associate. Lack of well-being in children increases the social (and financial) burden that the next generation has to carry. In very significant ways, it represents the antithesis of social progress. Personally, I really do actively enjoy being involved in doing the exact opposite of all that.

Someone not mentioned yet, who began working in the background while we were still carrying out casework from the enormous portacabin on the nastiest bend in Morning Lane, is group manager, Brigitte Jordaan. An entirely extraordinary person, and my latest guiding light, she combines an unfailing cheerfulness, energy and appetite for the difficulties faced by children and their families with a coruscating wit, a generosity of heart and a patience with our efforts and development that seem to verge on the superhuman. I'm sure she's got her down sides. The truth is that I'm not interested in them. I can think of no greater compliment or encouragement than the one she delivered to me the other day, when I was making some coffee for myself and Jeremy: 'Charlie, you keep me on my toes.' When people like Brigitte are moving fast within a model like the one outlined in this book, it's sometimes hard to be critical of its failings, because failings are an inevitable part of the learning process. Science proceeds on the basis that if you really can't prove something is wrong, or not working – a hypothesis, an idea, a perspective, a treatment, an intervention plan – then it must at least be the best solution for the present. Reclaiming Social Work's practitioners continue to test the hypotheses, to interrogate the terms by which they have been constructed, to 'perturb the system' as systems oriented practice would have it.

The way it seems…

There are many other stories from children's practitioners besides this one. Mine seems a legitimate and truthful tale to me because it gathers together a narrative that I personally find convincing. I've set out the truth in the facts I've identified as such, although there are certainly other facts that could be inferred or deducted from this, or in any other story. I've constructed perspectives that ring true to me and fit the circumstances that I have presented, and as I have understood them. I've quizzed myself and the diversities of the Reclaiming Social Work model throughout the development of my practice, to formulate both a sense of my own identity as a worker in the field and a sense of the direction in which my organisation and the work we are undertaking seems to be headed. Other truths and other stories would certainly find better relevance to the issues governing the circumstances that bring our service users to us. Other truths and other developments will be more significant to the development of their capacity to change in a way that addresses the circumstances outlined in the initial social services referral. Colleagues from different backgrounds, with different remits and different perspectives on themselves, the work they do and the people they do it with, will all produce other stories.

If I seem to have encountered individuals whose parts in my story are implausibly significant – and I can only say that I feel very fortunate indeed to have met and worked with them, and continue to do so – then I've certainly missed out many more people for whom there isn't space, or who don't seem to fit the limited intentions of this chapter from the perspective of a children's practitioner. Reclaiming Social Work in

Hackney is a gestalt.[4] If it seems to me that, at times, I've been indulged by having the privilege to work with 'the best' (which is Mark's definition of Brigitte), when other practitioners were or felt less fortunate, then I hope this story will focus a light on some new possibilities.

For me, the role of children's practitioner encompasses the very heart of effective social work practice, while Reclaiming Social Work provides the contextual paradigm, one around which other practitioners, panels, the procedures and processes, the collaborations and distinctions, the legal, medical, educational and administrative frameworks form a constellation that stands for the rules that society and living at least ask us to live by. Not simply by inviting and maintaining 'the voice of the child' in the work we do together, but because it involves finding a bridge in understanding between the very complex processes of society, and the realities that occur in the mind of a child with very significant needs.

If their safety depends on our feeling capable enough to share the details of our work openly and honestly with trusted colleagues, then it also requires a delicacy of sentiment and a consideration of children's capacities to ensure they don't become overloaded, in a way that undermines their own capacity to think. And to feel willing to share and join forces in drawing out the benefits of that thinking. All of which means that holding one's own as a children's practitioner, despite the very best support and guidance, requires very considerable resilience and flexibility if you're going to remain on your feet, and deliver an effective service to those with most need. Those, I should add, with the most justifiable reasons for expecting and hoping that those needs will be met.

If you've found this chapter difficult to read, what with the crag hopping between theory and practice, the names of people who seem related like a kind of family but whose roles shift about in response to circumstances, if you've also found the somewhat unrelenting positivity

---

4   The aggregate outcome of the various practices and perspectives outlined in this book is difficult to determine and describe in isolation. Reclaiming articulates a complex, layered responsive practice engaging with the particular characteristics and presenting issues associated with the population in which it operates. To say that its properties comprise more than the sum of its parts is simply to express its principal mode of action: a treatment paradigm for the consequences of poverty on children, rather than an operational manual for the minimisation of the harms that they inevitably experience. Reclaiming Social Work comprises an ethical approach to those aspects of social health affecting children and families, in line with the medical ethics that govern the development and implementation of interventions associated with biological well-being. In doing so, it makes prospective steps towards new patterns of governance well outside its own field – in health, in education, in law and in social policy.

a little unsettling, then please allow me to offer a qualified apology. Children's social care is unable to guarantee children's safety. To achieve such an odd and frankly unhealthy outcome would involve depriving them, and those personally responsible for their care, of their liberty. Instead, we seek to arrive at a position of 'safe uncertainty' where circumstances are on balance sufficiently secure to obviate unnecessary risk, while providing opportunities for children to grow, learn, explore and develop substantially meaningful and enjoyable relationships with the world they find, and with the people in it. That work makes demands on us of course, but also on the families with whom we work. It's that quality of collaborative effort that I've tried to replicate here. If this chapter hasn't made demands on you, then something's gone wrong. All the same, I've enjoyed setting out my developing experiences of Reclaiming Social Work as a children's practitioner, and hope you have too. If it's all been a bit of a stretch, then perhaps the stretch has been beneficial.

But it's also worth mentioning, I think, that aside from these sober matters, the other part of working as a children's practitioner involves making a mess with paints and paper, climbing trees, swinging on swings, persisting with grim days that turn out better in the end, or during the following week, or suddenly change their complexion because of a colleague's intelligent, kindly meant and well chosen words, or a child's smile. It's about finding ways to hear terrible things so that the telling of them, by a child to a person with an interest, supercedes the awful, lonely experience of living through them without sufficient hope to cope with the consequences. If children represent the future – and why shouldn't they, along with all the other things that people undertake speculatively – then for me at least, my experiences as a children's practitioner seem representative of the beginning of the story that is the future of children and young people's social work.

References

Barnard, A., Horner, N. and Wild, J. (eds) (2008) *Value Base of Social Work and Social Care: An Active Learning Handbook.* Maidenhead: Open University Press.

Bateson, G. (2000) *Steps to an Ecology of Mind: Collected Essays in Anthropology, Psychiatry, Evolution, and Epistemology.* Chicago, IL: University of Chicago Press.

Munro, E. (2011) *The Munro Review of Child Protection: Interim Report. The Child's Journey.* London: Department for Education. Available at www.education.gov.uk/munroreview/downloads/Munrointerimreport.pdf, accessed on 19 August 2011.

CHAPTER 12

Conclusion and Reflections on Our Journey

Isabelle Trowler and Steve Goodman

This is the final chapter of a book which we hope has shed some light on what Reclaiming Social Work means in terms of our social work values and how that translates into effective, evidenced-based practice. Consultant practitioners and their practice coaches have described through a series of case examples and personal commentaries the approaches taken within the model. To finish, then, we write a little about our experience as leaders and say some more about the many people who have helped us realise our vision. Implementation of Reclaiming Social Work is a major change programme, and one that we hold very close to our hearts. It is undoubtedly a story of relationships and relentless passion and pursuit of something most important to us.

Having practised, managed and led statutory social work services for a number of years, and by some fluke of circumstance, Steve and I found ourselves working with each other in the London Borough of Hackney at 205 Morning Lane. This chapter describes our story of how Reclaiming Social Work was created and implemented. It explains our starting position and why we took the journey that we did. It raises, we hope, some pertinent strategies for survival in the political environment of the local authority, survival in a high risk child protection context where serious concerns about practice were commonplace, and survival through a major change process. It discusses the nature of our professional partnership and the relationships we nurtured and leant on throughout this quiet revolution. It explores how we made friends with enemies, argued relentlessly about everything, and describes the moment when we realised that Reclaiming Social Work was going to live and breathe way beyond our involvement.

Having met in 2005 we started to explore forensically how we as leaders could enable good social work practice to flourish, despite the national crisis within the profession. When we began our journey we were certainly a lone local authority voice in our critical analysis of what was wrong with the system within which support to our most vulnerable and at-risk children was being delivered. While there have always been many individuals who shared our view, it was the willingness to take a principled and organisational stand on not only what was wrong, but what needed doing, which made our position unique. There was no national vision for what statutory children's social care should do and achieve. The failure to articulate that always meant disaster from the start, not least because academic institutions were not being guided carefully enough in what they were being funded to teach. Even with some inconsistent sense of what the curriculum should be, the intellectual ability of students accepted onto social work degree courses was not generally high enough, and many did not have the requisite academic or personal qualities needed to develop the skills set required to do the job of a children's social worker successfully. Over the previous decade and in an attempt to manage this widespread skills deficit a national system of performance management and centralised bureaucracy had emerged with many unintended consequences. The focus on risk assessment and management had been lost among a more generic, holistic approach to need and very little effective direct work was taking place which was skilled enough to effect positive change in families. With greater reliance on a procedural approach to professional practice, and ICT (information and communications technology) systems solutions, a workforce often incapable of professional, creative and independent thinking had emerged.

The profession suffered from a conveyor belt, risk-averse mentality to the inevitable detriment of the children and families it sought to serve. As practitioners were further and further removed from any sense of their own responsibility, or capability to effect positive change, or sense of professional pride, a dangerous casualness emerged, where even automated tasks were often done badly.

We stated from the beginning that it was our intention to reclaim social work and change what it had become. While an important structural change helped mark a fundamental different way of working, the real challenge was to change the professional culture described above. This meant creating very different ways of thinking about what was happening in families and why, and different ways of working directly with families to create positive and sustainable change. This required a very different skills set from that which was encouraged among employers and developed through qualifying courses. It also required social workers to share an ethical position on when the state needed to take a coercive role in the protection of children and the way in which that should be done.

When we speak in public we often refer to a particular defining moment when both Steve and I were sitting in his office, poring over our latest draft of what we referred to as the 'social work offer'. It was the usual management attempt at tampering with the periphery of the problem (pay and conditions, training opportunities, management competence). We tried to be enthusiastic and consider it a job well done but our hearts just weren't in it. We knew that it would change nothing, such was the scale of the problem we were being paid to fix. That day we struck a partnership deal that has since changed the course of both our lives. We agreed that we could not spend the rest of our careers overseeing mediocre social work, which frequently led to the decimation of family life, often without any serious attempt to keep children with their families. We come from very different social classes and have hugely different life experiences and that has since provoked many a heated discussion over the years we have worked together, but our shared political beliefs in the pivotal role of family (for better or for worse) and the necessity for minimum state intervention, and our deep-seated dislike of paperwork, process, time wasting, unfocused chatter and low energy managerial solutions, has held us in good stead for some of the storms we have weathered. In that meeting we agreed to try to find a way to make a radical and better plan to practise, manage and lead children's statutory social work in England. On reflection, for us personally and professionally, as well as, we think, for children's social work, this, our first decision, was our most profound decision within the Reclaiming Social Work journey.

We then worked for several months on our own and behind closed doors, working out the detail of the model, and I mean the detail. We worked out numbers and caseloads and financial implications and roles and reasons not to do it and reasons why it was the only thing to do.

There was, however, a third person in this relationship without whom Reclaiming Social Work would not have got off the ground. While our number crunching and debate went raging on, Debra Philip, our head of Family Support, was leading the way from the front. Debra was a social worker and a systemic family therapist. She had joined Hackney to lead the Therapeutic Intervention Service for looked-after children a couple of years previously, and Steve had forged a strong and close relationship with her, recognising the talent, energy and thoughtful way she engaged the world, moving her closer and closer to him through the hierarchy. Debra was like no other person before or since. Her constant seeking for professional treasure was her trade mark. She shared our perspective on family and the role of the state, but she offered a skills set that neither Steve nor I had – patience and understanding of a myriad of different positions, each of which she gave equal respect. Debra drew us up short when we were badly behaved; she forced us to think again and again and was never once defeated. Very sadly, Debra died in 2010. This book is dedicated to Debra, so that her enormous contribution will never be forgotten.

During 2006 Debra arranged for some systemic practitioners to move into Access and to work alongside our duty social workers. This was another defining moment. Within weeks, our numbers of looked-after children started to fall. Now we knew we were on to something big. The difference this made to statutory social work practice was striking. The clinical staff were some of the best, some still working with us today, forming the vanguard of what has become a thriving additional skills set to this often-fraught context. We often use the phrase, 'slowing down to speed up'. When an over-stretched duty social worker goes out on an initial visit, for example, to try to prevent an adolescent coming into care because the family can no longer cope with their behaviour, invariably the social worker returns to the office *with* the adolescent. That same scenario, but where the social worker is accompanied by an experienced and confident clinical practitioner armed with a different set of engagement skills, a strengths-based and respectful approach towards the family, and a brief to find a solution, started to result in a different and safe outcome for children. The detail of our systems and practice methodology is set out in Chapter 2; the message we want the reader to take from this chapter, however, is that leadership behaviours, at all levels of the organisation, are the most powerful change agent, and the most important of those is that demonstrated by the practitioner as they lead the family towards a different way of being.

We were heavily influenced by the concept of Malcolm Gladwell's tipping point (Gladwell 2000) (we liked this man mostly for making a success out of spending endless working hours in New York cafes) and we knew for Reclaiming Social Work to take off we needed to locate brave, innovative, creative, dynamic personalities, to form the critical mass we needed at a practice and management level. A key survival strategy, not perhaps as intentional at the time as we would now recommend, was to surround ourselves internally and externally with a small army of like-minded people, all wanting to do *the right thing*. This included those who helped us think through the evidence base for effective interventions, most notably Professor Stephen Scott from King's College London, other academics including Professor David Shemmings from the University of Kent and Professor Donald Forrester from the University of Bedfordshire. We spent as much time as needed with our director, lead member and chief executive to persuade them of the need to let us implement the model. We spent a whole day with our director, just the three of us, and Steve and I took seven hours of non-stop questions.

Once we got the political go-ahead we did even more searching. We searched far and wide, using all our contacts, and favours off old friends to source people who would come and try their luck within our new world. We met with journalists, young people in care, we commissioned focus groups of social workers across London to tell us what they thought of the model, not saying which authority it was because we knew it would skew results because of Hackney's reputational lag; we commissioned more workshops and asked why social workers wouldn't practise in Hackney, so we could get a good perspective on what we would need to do to change minds. Then we spoke to our staff. We held four conferences and all staff came. Here we unveiled our plans and held our breath while we waited for the room to erupt. And astoundingly staff clapped. They didn't shout, or get cross about yet more change or worry instantly about their futures or rail against the model. They clapped. And they did this because they could see that this was not a cost-cutting measure; it wasn't about re-arranging the deck chairs. They recognised that we were really serious about changing their working context so we could together help change families' lives.

Following on from that and as we launched the change programme we spoke at conferences and workshops across the country; everywhere we made friends and one or two enemies on the way. The country was ripe for debate about social work effectiveness, the evils of the performance management culture and how beleaguered the profession felt. We also set up our project team, which was instrumental in getting things off the ground and driving the detail through to operational delivery. Clare Chamberlain and Steve had worked together years ago in Leicestershire and he suggested she come and see me with a view to coming to help out. I spoke to Clare for about an hour, after which she said rather gravely that she would need to think about it and get back to me. This was late on in the afternoon. The next morning, almost before dawn broke, she was back on the phone, saying she had consulted many far and wide (and now knowing Clare very well, I know that she would have indeed done exactly that), and was going to chance it and join us as our project manager. She committed to a year on the spot and arrived shortly afterwards.

Having Clare with us was hugely important and demonstrates the well-known need for different personalities and skills sets in any team. Clare was the frequent arbitrator between Steve and me; she was not phased by our bitter battles, or complete inability to compromise with each other. Steve and I had offices directly opposite each other and she would literally move across from one room to the other, repeatedly explaining to one what the other needed to have said without the accompanied heckling cacophony of protest. In fact, she facilitated each exchange to its intellectual end, through which the better argument won the war. So often in these grand designs the pressure to compromise emerges and threatens to undo the original intention. I can't remember doing that once and I think the model reflects that. It is intellectually sound and logical to its core. And we needed Clare to help us get there – to contain our egos. She was our very own super ego. But she did many other things too – she did the casework maths, some complicated transfer scheme of case allocation so we didn't lose track of any children during the transition phase (a system which I still don't understand); she wrote report after report to feed the political machine. She spent hours reassuring those whose jobs were at risk and those who failed our infamous verbal reasoning tests. She listened to the fury of those who had provided Hackney with 20 years of hard labour but who were now being told there was no longer room for them at the table. She helped people leave the organisation, ensuring that people felt that at least someone had listened. Clare did the detail, the stuff neither Steve nor I had the patience to do justice, but which was critical to the model's success.

Another key player in our team was Mary Jackson. Thank goodness for Mary. The best thing about Mary was that she wasn't a social worker! Mary knew about advertising and recruitment campaigns, she had a natural international perspective, she knew about private business and media contacts; she didn't know how a local authority worked and therefore was never constrained by that knowledge. So she provided solutions with drive and simplicity. She was our new blood, unrestricted by political fear. Mary got things done. At times the corporate centre seemed to be our corporate enemy; everything we wanted to do, it seemed as though someone was getting paid to stop us doing it. Mary found loop-holes, argued hard, was steadfast in her resolve and never once let us down. She was the pinnacle of our much-valued approach to trusting employee–employer relationships. If you start from a position of trust, that people can and do want to do a good job for you, it is only by exception that people won't deliver. It's not that people won't make mistakes, by forgetting or misjudging or being late or misunderstanding, but almost all instances of error are simple mistakes and must be treated as such. It's a principle we hold dear and have always put into practice in our leadership. However, if someone is dangerously thoughtless or reckless, time wasting or disrespectful to families, that was an entirely different matter, and rarely would people, in these circumstances, be offered a second chance.

In the corporate centre's defence, what reason did they have to be confident that we knew what we were doing? We were taking a radical new departure from the traditional recruitment strategies and selection methods. We wanted to design our own adverts and refused to adhere to the line on corporate colours. Sometimes we just did things, knowing we might get into trouble, but we took our chances and most of the time it didn't backfire. Looking back on that period, the need for restriction and rules comes into sharp relief. Frankly if the whole organisation acted as we did, all at the same time, it would be chaos. The truth is we were ahead of the game and were allowed to be maverick. We were running so fast, the junior bureaucrats didn't have a chance of catching us, and those more senior than us let us run. Why? Because at the same time as changing at top speed, we kept the ship afloat. Our performance indicators were good, we kept out of the press, inspection outcomes were not too bad, but critically our budgets were in line, and most importantly, the faster we ran the more money we saved. Over the three years of implementation we released huge efficiencies, year on year. Now who was going to stop us doing that?

There are some key elements for any successful change programme, some of which we identify here, and we know that much has been written about leadership and to what degree it can be taught or whether it is something innate. We really don't know the answer to that and would not wish to compete with those who have studied the subject for years, but we do know what worked for our organisation. We were always focused, driven by the need to stop families being unnecessarily torn apart, we had fun, we didn't work long hours, we knew almost everyone working for us, we were visible and in general respected if not always liked.

We privileged each new unit in every way; no unit was allowed to go live unless we knew it would be successful, that the right complement of skill and expertise was present. Staff didn't get our much-prized training and development opportunities until they were placed in a unit, and in general the best were placed first. There were some pretty difficult periods. After about 12 months the organisational energy dipped. The high of the natural drama created by change was lowered and we were having trouble recruiting consultant social workers. There was increasing tension between those working in teams who felt second class and second best, and the units flying high on a mixture of nervous energy, media attention and the freedom to practise in a way that meant change for families was not only possible but frequently inevitable. There was a lot of pressure from some of the heads of service to change tact, to offer the same input into temporary staff, to start more units more quickly and to lower the bar for entry. There was no shortage of applications for consultants – we had literally hundreds for 48 posts – but many just couldn't make it through the testing. To have changed approach at that point would have been disastrous so we didn't cave in and create a lower threshold but we did start to search further afield. We knew that over half of the consultants we had recruited were trained abroad, although most had substantial UK practice experience (today Hackney still has a high proportion of consultants trained abroad). Everyone on the child protection front line knows that newly qualified social workers are ill prepared and the amount of time dedicated to specific skills training is severely limited, and yet the national debate about curriculum content for both pre and post-qualifying courses seems the hardest to influence, so we travelled to the US to try our luck and came home with ten new recruits. Six months later they were with us. On reflection it's probably not a strategy we would deploy again. It was resource intensive, and while some consultants are still with us today and doing a great job, others have fallen by the wayside, disappointed by their mis-interpretation or our mis-representation of how things would be.

In any event something else had started to happen. The Reclaiming Social Work profile started to take off. We had previously had quite a lot of press coverage but now something much more powerful and un-anticipated emerged. Through word of mouth, the Reclaiming Social Work word was starting to spread, what Professor Shemmings would describe to us as the viral effect. Many had been watching and waiting. The interim evaluation report came out, led by Professor Munro from LSE, that gave some very positive early messages about what was happening in Hackney:

> Taken together, data indicate that Reclaiming Social Work is having an overall positive effect on the *management of risk*, the *quality of care* and the *response to families*, when compared to previous practice both at Hackney and elsewhere.

> Reclaiming Social Work enables better learning systems, more opportunity for critical reflection, a more appropriate mix of skills in dealing with families and a better balance between meeting performance indicator targets and responding to family needs professionally. When compared with previous practice, Reclaiming Social Work shows an improved approached to decision-making in child protection, and improved approach in interaction with families and other professionals, fewer constraints on practice and better prioritization and consistency of care. (Munro 2009, emphasis in original)

The organisational energy re-emerged, and talented, skilled and interested practitioners started to emerge too. While we had always been cynical about the level of children's social work practice skill available on the London labour market, there had been points at which we thought even we had been seriously over-optimistic! Over the next 18 months, however, we recruited more and more people and then the moment arrived when we knew we had cracked it. The tipping point had truly happened. We were home and dry. Over this implementation period, and as a new skills set emerged, the numbers of children in the public care system had steadily declined, from about 470 to 270; re-referral rates were declining and children in care proceedings fell very significantly too. The time it took us to conclude proceedings fell by 30 per cent. Staff sickness levels, something that had plagued us for years, fell a dramatic 50 per cent. Critically, though, as a practice system, we acted as a whole. By the summer 2010 we had all units up and running and an unprecedented creative energy had been established across the organisation.

People always ask what we would have done differently, in hindsight. When we were first asked this question we always appeared a bit dumbstruck and to our detriment, that still seems to be the case; I suppose a further indicator of our steadfast belief in ourselves and our staff and the system we created. Our story is that most of what we did worked very well and most of our decisions were the right ones made at the right time. Chapter 11 is written by Charlie Clayton, a children's practitioner and now a trainee social worker who has been with us for most of the change period. We asked him to write the change story from an employee perspective, in recognition of our belief that there is always more than one truth. It is entirely our failing that we cannot muster even a few strategic errors.

Implementing Reclaiming Social Work was hard work, frustrating, sometimes exhilarating and ultimately very rewarding. It has created a critical mass of highly intelligent, thoughtful and committed practitioners enthused by this different way of working and constantly encouraged by each other's presence. Its initial impact on families is demonstrated through evaluation reports, external case review and perhaps, in particular, the frequent letters we receive from professionals and families offering thanks for the work practitioners have done.

There is always more to do. We are still forging ahead, spreading the word about what we believe to be the most effective system for child protection social work. In the meantime we continue to move forward, with determination and passion for our work, hope for the social work profession and the families it supports.

Reference

Gladwell, M. (2000) *The Tipping Point: How Little Things Can Make a Big Difference.* New York: Abacus.

Munro, E. (2009) *Reclaiming Social Work: Early Findings.* London: Cross, Hubbard and Munro.

List of Contributors

Isabelle Trowler and **Steve Goodman** are both qualified social workers and the architects of Reclaiming Social Work. Having worked together for several years in Hackney as Assistant Director and Deputy Director, they now work together in their social enterprise, Morning Lane Associates, dedicated to changing the way child and family social work operates in the UK.

Charlie Clayton is a trainee social worker and practises in Hackney as a Children's Practitioner within a Reclaiming Social Work unit for children in need and those subject to child protection plans. He has an interest in psychology and the natural sciences. Charlie had an extended spell in broadcasting, then a brief trajectory through remedial education with children and young people, eventually leading him to train in social work.

Timo Dobrowolski is a German social pedagogue/social worker from the maritime city of Hamburg. He graduated there as a nursery school teacher prior to his social work studies, and now practises in Hackney as a Consultant Social Worker. He has led Reclaiming Social Work units in Access and Assessment and Looked After Children Services. Previous experiences included working in psychiatric day care and with young people who self-harm.

Karen Gaughan grew up in Blackpool. She studied English and Theology at Sheffield University and has an MA in Social Work from Liverpool University. Since 2000, she has held various roles in children's social care and youth justice settings in Liverpool, Bootle, Sunderland, Newcastle, Islington and Haringey. Rejuvenated through Reclaiming Social Work, she has spent the last three years practising in Hackney as a Consultant Social Worker. Despite her hometown, she hates roller coasters.

Steve Goodman has a BA in Psychology from the University of Hull, an MA in Social Work, and an MBA from Leicester University. He has had extensive experience in the field of social care and began his career in Leicestershire, originally as a front-line social worker and then in a range of managerial and senior strategic roles. Steve has a strong track record of reducing numbers of children in public care through strengthening effective, evidence-based support to families. Steve sits on the Scientific Advisory Board of the National Academy of Parenting Research.

Sonya Kalyniak qualified as a social worker in Canada and has lived in the UK since 2004. As a Consultant Social Worker, she has led Reclaiming Social Work units for Looked After Children Services. After a number of years at the front line, she is currently working in Hackney to incorporate organisational learning into social work practice. Sonya's ongoing ambitions are to improve health and well-being and to master the French language.

Rick Mason was born in Canada but raised in England. He has a BA degree in Philosophy, is a father of two teenage sons and lives in Hackney, where he has worked as a social worker for nearly 25 years. He practises as a Consultant Social Worker and leads a Reclaiming Social Work unit for children in public care.

Stewart McCafferty gained a first degree in Social Science from the University of York, followed by a Master's degree in Social Work, studying under Martin Herbert. He is qualified as a supervisor and trainer in systemic psychotherapy. He has trained in eye movement desensitisation and reprocessing, and has a particular interest in evidence-based practice with attachment issues. Stewart is Director of Social Learning Consultants Ltd and Clinical Consultant with The Attachment Practice.

Nick Pendry was born and brought up in London. He completed a degree in Politics at the University of Hull and an MSc in Social Work at the University of Kent. He completed his clinical training in Family and Systemic Psychotherapy at the Institute of Family Therapy and Birkbeck College, University of London. He was Head of Professional Practice within the Reclaiming model, and now practises at Great Ormond Street Hospital and works with the Institute of Family Therapy, Morning Lane Associates and other local authorities that promote systemic approaches to child protection practice. He lives in South London, is married, has two children and loves to play tennis.

Martin Purbrick is a qualified social worker and led one of the first Reclaiming Social Work units in Hackney as a Consultant Social Worker. He studied Social Work at Middlesex University as a mature student. He lives in North London close to his beloved Arsenal Football Club with his wife Vicki and daughter Isla. In his spare time, he enjoys walking, especially in the mountains, despite suffering from vertigo.

Julie Rooke led one of the first Reclaiming Social Work units in Hackney as a Consultant Social Worker. She now practises at Great Ormond Street Hospital and works with Morning Lane Associates. Julie was born and brought up in Toronto, Canada, and did her first degree in Biology and Psychology. She has a Master's in Social Work from the University of Toronto and came to the UK in 2003.

Karen Schiltroth qualified as a social worker in Canada and recently completed an MSc in Mental Health Social Work with Children at King's College London. She has worked in children's social care in the UK for eight years, and led one of the first Reclaiming Social Work units in Hackney as a Consultant Social Worker. She now has the lead for professional development across the council's Children's Services. Having started her academic life studying physics, she is particularly interested in the way structures and systems shape human relationships.

Stephen Scott is a Consultant Child Psychiatrist at the Maudsley Hospital, where he works in a multidisciplinary team alongside social workers in the National Adoption and Fostering Clinic. Here, a wide range of childcare cases are assessed and interventions are offered. Stephen is also Professor of Child Health and Behaviour at the Institute of Psychiatry, King's College London, and Director of Research and Development for the National Academy for Parenting Research. He is the National Director of the Multidimensional Treatment Foster Care project and Fostering Changes programme, which has been disseminated nationally with its second edition manual launched.

David Shemmings, PhD, is Professor of Social Work at the University of Kent and Visiting Professor of Child Protection Research at Royal Holloway, University of London. David is the author of numerous publications, his most recent being a work focusing on disorganised attachment. Currently, David leads the Advanced Child Protection stream in West London and the Assessment of Disorganised Attachment and Maltreatment (ADAM) project across the UK.

Yvonne Shemmings, MA, CQSW, DMS, is a continuing professional development consultant and has trained child protection professionals in over 30 organisations over the past 15 years. Her specialisms are attachment theory and direct work with children. She is a registered social worker and was a senior manager in social services.

Isabelle Trowler qualified as a social worker from the LSE in 1996 and has since worked within the voluntary and statutory sectors in education and social care settings. She has worked as a front-line practitioner, a commissioner of children's services and, in the last ten years, as a senior manager in Kensington and Chelsea and in Hackney. Isabelle has most recently worked as an advisor to the Munro Independent Review of Child Protection, and is part of the government's Working Group on implementation.

Index